W9-CBN-568

UNEMPLOYMENT AND PRIMARY COMMODITY PRICES

Unemployment and Primary Commodity Prices

Theory and Evidence in a Global Perspective

Annalisa Cristini
Associate Professor in Economics
University of Bergamo
Italy

Foreword by Stephen Nickell

First published in Great Britain 1999 by
MACMILLAN PRESS LTD
Houndmills, Basingstoke, Hampshire RG21 6XS and London
Companies and representatives throughout the world

A catalogue record for this book is available from the British Library.

ISBN 0–333–74833–6

First published in the United States of America 1999 by
ST. MARTIN'S PRESS, INC.,
Scholarly and Reference Division,
175 Fifth Avenue, New York, N.Y. 10010

ISBN 0–312–22036–7

Library of Congress Cataloging-in-Publication Data
Cristini, Annalisa, 1961–
Unemployment and primary commodity prices : theory and evidence in
a global perspective / Annalisa Cristini ; foreword by Stephen
Nickell.
p.   cm.
Includes bibliographical references and index.
ISBN 0–312–22036–7 (cloth)
1. Unemployment—OECD countries—Mathematical models.   2. Primary
commodities—Prices—OECD countries—Mathematical models.
3. Petroleum products—Prices—OECD countries—Mathematical models.
I. Title.
HD5707.5.C753   1999
331.13'7—dc21   98–44643
                                                              CIP

This book is printed on paper suitable for recycling and made from fully managed and
sustained forest sources.

10   9   8   7   6   5   4   3   2   1
08   07   06   05   04   03   02   01   00   99

Printed and bound in Great Britain by
Antony Rowe Ltd, Chippenham, Wiltshire

To Luigi

Contents

List of Tables

List of Figures

Acknowledgments

This book ensues from my Oxford DPhil thesis which I wrote under the supervision of Professor Stephen Nickell. Although the basic ideas developed in the thesis remain, this book is the result of further efforts: overall the topic has been investigated in greater detail, a description of the facts has been provided together with more extensive statistics; the theoretical model itself has been revised and the empirical analysis updated.

My most generous thanks go to Stephen Nickell. I learned a lot from him as a student and afterwards; tenaciously he kept reading the numerous drafts of the book and always gave me stimulating advices and sharp comments.

I also wish to thank Piero Ferri who has been the supervisor of my undergraduate thesis at the University of Bergamo; he never stopped encouraging me to complete this work.

I am also obliged to Richard Layard, Edmund Phelps, Robert Bacon and Christopher Gilbert, for interesting discussions and stimulating ideas; to David Vines and Andrew Glyn, who had been the external examiners of my DPhil thesis; to Daphne Nicolitsas, who read a draft of the manuscript.

Finally, this book has also improved from the comments of two anonymous referees who suggested important revisions on an earlier draft.

Foreword

This book is based on an Oxford DPhil thesis which I supervised and which was completed in the late 1980s.

The idea is to explain unemployment across the OECD, treating the OECD countries as one unit. Such aggregation will, of course, lose some of the fine detail but there are significant gains. Over the last three decades, there have been dramatic fluctuations in unemployment in all the OECD countries, with unemployment being substantially higher today than it was 30 years ago in all of them. Furthermore, the fluctuations themselves are highly correlated. As a consequence it is commonplace to find that explanations of unemployment in any one country depend, at least in part, on the level of economic activity in the rest of the world. In the early 1980s, the 'world recession' was blamed for the then parlous state of more or less every OECD economy.

But this is hardly a deep explanation because, once we add up all the countries, it is no explanation at all. The fundamental problem is, what caused the world recession in the first place? And this is best answered by analysing the world.

We can start with a simple fact. The correlation between the OECD unemployment rate and primary commodity prices over the period 1954–91 is 0.94. This is extraordinarily high and is not just the result of both series being simple trends. So the suggestion must be that primary commodity prices are part of the story.

This led to an initial investigation of the OECD bloc, treating primary commodity prices as exogenous. This turned out not to be good enough, because the obvious feedback from OECD activity to commodity prices was too large to be ignored. So the next strategy was to split commodity prices into oil and non-oil, taking only the former as exogenous. Here the ground is a bit firmer because many of the major fluctuations in the oil price are driven by forces other than OECD economic activity. However, the need to explain non-oil commodity prices leads inexorably to a more detailed analysis of the non-OECD bloc, and the inclusion of key factors such as non-OECD debt and world real interest rates.

The model set out in what follows is about as far as it is possible to go while retaining the ability to see what is going on. It is, perhaps, a shade complicated but it repays study and produces many insights. To find out more, read on!

Stephen Nickell
University of Oxford

1 Introduction

The OECD rate of unemployment and primary commodity prices appear to be inextricably linked. As shown in Figure 1.1 the positive correlation is striking: both variables are roughly constant around the mean until 1972; thereafter they undergo two notable upward jumps in 1973 and again 1979 and finally fall in 1985–86. Between 1954 and 1991 the correlation index is as high as 0.94.

The relationship between some measure of industrial activity and the development of primary commodity prices has been observed by other scholars before: Hamilton (1983) presents a picture showing the correlation between US recessions and oil price changes; IMF (1985) relates the cycles of the industrial production in major industrial economies with the changes in the price of primary commodities.

Although this correlation is quite engaging, it does not, of course, prove the existence of a causal link between primary commodity prices and the OECD rate of unemployment. In fact, if one distinguishes between the oil and the non-oil

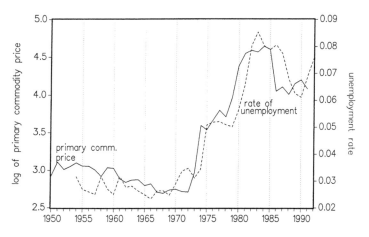

Figure 1.1   OECD rate of unemployment and primary commodity prices

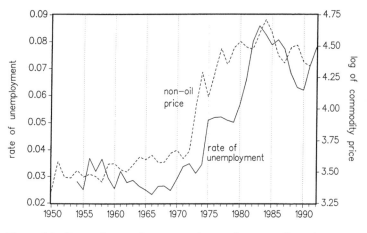

Figure 1.2   Rate of unemployment and non-oil commodity prices

component of primary commodity prices, it turns out that it is especially the oil component that closely tracks the path of the rate of unemployment though low-frequency movements of non-oil commodity prices also move in line with it (Figures 1.2 and 1.3). Moreover, if we shift from nominal to real commodity prices, the correlation between non-oil prices and the rate of

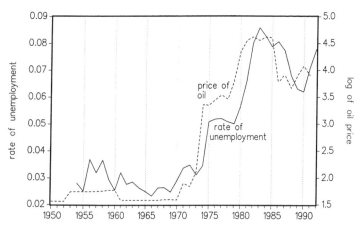

Figure 1.3   Rate of unemployment and the price of oil

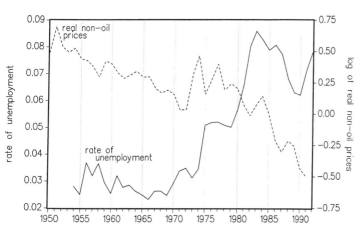

Figure 1.4 Rate of unemployment and real non-oil commodity prices

unemployment seems to vanish whereas the relationship between the oil price and the rate of unemployment clearly persists (Figures 1.4 and 1.5). Further, a closer look at Figures 1.3 and 1.5 indicates that the remarkable turning points of the oil price (that is 1973, 1979, 1986) typically precede, by a year or less, those of the rate of unemployment. This fact, which

Figure 1.5 Rate of unemployment and the real oil price

could indicate some causality running from the price of oil to the rate of unemployment, has also been previously observed and investigated.[1]

Indeed the exceptional 1970s oil shocks prompted several studies on the relationship between primary commodity prices and the economic performance of industrialized countries. However, the standard framework, based on partial equilibrium models, typically neglected the potential feedbacks between primary commodity prices and the economic activity of the industrialized countries, while the alternative multi-country models, by accounting for the numerous links within the world economy, easily reached huge dimensions and a high degree of complexity.

This book tries to overcome the drawbacks of the partial equilibrium approach without loosing grasp of the interactions between the economic variables. By adopting the so-called bloc approach, we build a comprehensive though empirically tractable macroeconomic model; the latter is used to inquire into the impressions suggested by the above pictures in order to understand the transmission mechanisms existing between the so-called North and South of the world[2] and, in particular, deepen the comprehension of the links between primary commodity prices and industrialized countries.

1.1 MODELLING THE LINKS BETWEEN PRIMARY COMMODITY PRICES AND THE OECD ECONOMY

The starting point of the analysis is the recognition that the industrialized countries as a whole virtually represent the demand side of the primary commodity market so that their performance is bound to strongly affect primary commodity prices. Moreover, the responsiveness of primary commodity prices to market forces (Labys, 1980) implies, for a large number of LDC, recurrent economic instabilities which, in turn, may easily spill over to the industrialized countries.

Kaldor (1976), for example, argues that 'any large change in commodity prices tends to have dampening effects on industrial activity'. His reasoning is based on the worsening of the LDC terms of trade and on the consequent reduction of OECD exports. According to this view even a rise of primary commodity prices is likely to worsen LDC terms of trade, because of the North's increased production costs, the appearance of wage resistance and eventually of restrictive policies aimed to contain inflation. The consequent recession dampens the demand of commodities from the North and quickly reverts the terms of trade against the South.[3]

Yet the trade channel, though studied from a long time, is not the only one which propagates the various impulses to the system; the financial market, in particular, has recently become one of the most important factors linking the world economies and this finds explicit recognition in this book.

1.1.1   The characteristics of the model and the bloc approach

A typical bloc model describes the world economy as the interplay of a set of worldwide markets;[4] Van Wijnbergen (1985) and Beenstock (1988) are significant examples of bloc models estimated on historical data; conceptually similar are also a few theoretical papers which look at North–South interaction (Kanbur and Vines, 1987, Moutos and Vines, 1989, 1992).

In particular we consider four principal blocs: the OECD economy, the LDC economy, the financial market and the primary commodity market; the choice of this highly aggregated approach, was prompted by three basic considerations.

First of all, bloc models allow the *joint* determination of primary commodity prices and economic activity, a requirement that any model aimed at analysing the relationship between these two variables must satisfy.

Second, these models ignore all intra-bloc trades which, in particular, implies that as long as primary commodity prices approximate the OECD average import price, they can fully account for the bloc's imported inflation. On the contrary, were imports within the OECD also allowed, the inflation imported by each country could be partly the consequence of the inflation exported by other members so that the sources of the price variability would be difficult to disentangle and could remain ultimately unexplained.

As shown in the Appendix to this chapter, the OECD real import unit value is directly proportional to an aggregated real primary commodity price index as long as: i) the proportion of imported primary commodities relative to imported manufactured goods is greater than the proportion between the same class of goods in gross output and ii) these proportions are constant. Although since 1970 industrialized countries have increased their self-sufficiency in primary commodities while tending to import a larger percentage of manufactured products from developing countries, the proportionality between the primary commodity price index and the import price index still holds.

The third reason that persuaded us to work with a bloc model is its small size relative to standard world macro-models; this makes it empirically manageable and permits a clearer understanding of the interactions in operation. Though these advantages are at the expense of the model's representativeness, we think that the specific objectives of this research make the bloc approach a convincing strategy.

1.2   PRIMARY COMMODITY PRICES: A HISTORICAL PERSPECTIVE

The purpose of this section is to equip the reader with some factual information on the role of primary commodities both for the industrialized and the developing countries. These two regions, though more and more interdependent, still show deep differences in terms of economic structure and these imply quite diverse impacts of primary commodities on their economic performances (see Table 1.1).

In 1963 almost 90 per cent of developing countries' total export receipts derived from primary commodities while, in the same period, this percentage was only around 30 per cent for

Table 1.1 Export composition: share of goods in total exports

	1963	1973	1979	1983	1987	1990	1991
World							
Total pr. commodities	45.3	37.7	40.5	39.5	28.4	26.6	24.9
Fuels	10.2	11.0	19.9	20.9	11.4	10.6	9.4
Manufactured	52.5	60.4	57.9	58.7	69.7	70.1	71.9
Industrialized countries							
Total pr. commodities	33.2	27.5	25.7	26.4	20.3	19.1	na
Fuels	4.0	3.5	5.9	8.0	4.4	4.2	na
Manufactured	64.4	70.9	72.7	72.0	77.9	77.3	na
Developing countries							
Total pr. commodities	87.3	77.4	78.7	70.6	50.5	48.6	na
Fuels	29.7	39.6	55.4	50.1	28.6	29.1	na
Manufactured	10.8	21.8	20.9	28.5	47.9	50.7	na

Source: GATT, Le Commerce International, 1987/88, 1990/91
Notes: The shares are computed on the value of exports in US $ bill.;
the percentages are on the total exports of each area.

the industrialized countries. Although the share of primary commodities in total exports declines, thereafter, in both regions, the export structures continue to show a significant discrepancy: in the late 1980s, primary commodities still constitute almost 50 per cent of the developing area total export revenues compared with a share of 20 per cent of the industrialized country exports. A detailed portrait of the South shows even more striking contrasts: in the mid-1970s the IMF registered 84 developing countries dependent on only a few commodity exports; specifically, a single commodity accounted for at least 30 per cent of the total export value for 75 per cent of these countries, for at least 50 per cent of the total export value for 43 per cent of these countries and for at least 70 per cent of the total export value for 27 per cent of these countries.

More recent figures provided by the World Bank (1994) show that in 1992 the low-income economy (excluding China and India) exports are still constituted by 40 per cent of fuels, minerals and metals and 21 per cent of other primary commodities. These shares are 34 per cent and 27 per cent for the severely indebted low- and middle-income countries and 7 per cent and 11 per cent for the high-income economies even including, in the latter, the United Arab Emirates. If we deem these figures with the evolution of the prices of primary commodities the role of the latter in shaping the world economy is clearly revealed.

It is by now well documented that, in the short run, primary commodity prices undergo substantially higher fluctuations relative to manufactured good prices and this is confirmed by the standard deviations of the de-trended price series reported in Table 1.2.[5] These sharp swings originate from the characteristics of the primaries themselves (highly homogeneous, short-run low elasticities of supply and demand) and, consequently, of the market that governs their price (usually

Table 1.2   Standard deviations of commodity prices and of the OECD GDP deflator

	1950–91	*1950–72*	*1973–91*
Non-oil primary comm.	0.215	0.190	0.188
Oil	0.610	0.589	0.519
Total primary comm.	0.417	0.440	0.318
OECD GDP deflator	0.121	0.140	0.080

Notes: i) The standard deviations are computed on de-trended prices; the latter are defined as the residuals obtained by regressing the logarithm of the price on a constant and a linear trend. ii) Definitions and sources are given in the data section.

highly competitive and strongly responsive to market conditions, with the exception of a few cases of cartels and international agreements).

For many countries this high degree of price flexibility is reflected in erratic export revenues; although the effects of the latter on the country's investments and growth is still an unsettled issue, the uncertainty surrounding what is, in most cases, the major component of a developing economy wealth, makes it difficult, for both the public and the private sector, to implement smooth and forward-looking policies.

The greater diversification of the industrialized countries' production and trade, together with the enforcement of stabilizing pricing policies (for example the European community agricultural policy) permits a more effective control of the direct impact of primary commodity price fluctuations; none the less the relationship between the developed countries' economic activity and primary commodity prices is substantial as they are the leading consumers and importers of primary products: in 1987 almost 70 per cent of primary commodities exported by the developing area were directed to the industrialized countries which also absorbed over 80 per cent of their own primary exports (GATT, 1987–88).

Economic interdependence between North and South as well as a growing interest in the primary commodity market as a conveyer of impulses from one economy to the other, were crucially spurred by the oil shocks of the 1970s. The main reason for this relates to the importance that fuels have gradually acquired for the industrialized countries and to the latter's heavy energy import dependency, largely satisfied by oil.[6] It is therefore useful to glance at the recent history of oil and at the link between oil and non-oil commodities.

1.3 THE OIL MARKET

Oil became the largest single source of commercial energy at the beginning of the 1950s for the United States, in the early 1960s for the Western countries and in 1967 for the world as a whole. However, until recently, there remained important differences from country to country: in the United Kingdom coal prevailed as the main source of energy until 1970, whereas in Eastern Europe and China it dominated until the mid-1980s. From the 1970s oil was also the principal energy source used by non-oil developing countries although their per-capita consumption was much lower than that of the developed countries.

In fact oil's attainment of this leading position among energy sources was a lengthy process; although systematic exploration for deep oil reservoirs began in the 1850s, in 1929 oil accounted for less than 15 per cent of the world energy consumption and 80 per cent was still supplied by coal. In the following decade, despite the great depression, there was a substantial rise in oil consumption in the USA where it covered 30 per cent of the energy requirement while remaining around 10 per cent in Europe. It was not until the aftermath of the Second World War that oil demand began to rise considerably: energy requirements dictated by the pressing needs for reconstruction and by the ensuing economic expansion could no longer be served by coal alone. Moreover, increased oil production and the discovery of new oil fields made the labour-intensive coal extraction less and less competitive.

The first decline of worldwide oil consumption since the end of World War II happened in 1974, in response to the exceptional price increase that occurred between October 1973 and January 1974. After a short recovery initiated in 1976, world oil consumption fell again between 1979 and 1980 in response to a further oil price rise; this time the drop of oil demand was so pronounced that it induced a decline of the world total energy consumption. Yet the expenditure on imported oil rose from 0.5 per cent of the world gross product to 2.5 per cent during the first oil shock, and to 5 per cent during the second oil shock.

1.3.1   The first oil shock

A mixture of market and political events are at the root of what is known as the first oil shock which resulted in a new balance of the world oil power and, more generally, in a new pattern of the world economic relations.

By the end of 1970 the oil market began to show signs of instability as the USA encountered severe supply shortage problems and their energy import dependence increased. This caused an increasing competition over energy supplies between the USA and the other oil-importing Western countries and these conflicting interests prevented the attainment of a concerted action despite a severe world energy crisis being commonly foreseen. Indeed, contrary to most Western countries, the USA, being also a chief oil producer, was ready to accept a bidding up of the oil price.

The 1973 winter oil demand tightened the oil market further and finally caused a worldwide rise of its market price. On the contrary, the Middle East oil posted prices, on which the Western oil-companies calculated taxes due to the oil-producing countries, remained well below the market prices. Consequently, the major gainers from this situation were the oil companies whose post-tax profits rose between 170 to 500 per cent from 1972 to October 1973.

The Organization of Petroleum Exporting Countries' (OPEC) reaction was to ask for an agreement to link posted prices to market prices and inflation. As oil companies, supported by oil-importing Western countries, resisted such a deal, OPEC, on 16 October 1973, unilaterally resolved to increase the posted price by 70 per cent. The following day the Arab oil-producing countries decided to adopt production cutbacks in support of the Middle East war intended to free the territories that Israeli had occupied since 1967.

The oil sanctions succeeded in magnifying the effects of supply shortages on oil prices and induced international initiatives in favour of the conflict; the sanctions were repealed in mid 1974. However, by January 1974 OPEC had become a major party in the world economy; the trade balance and political relations abruptly changed and oil-importing countries became aware of their vulnerable position. At the same time, the clash between Saudi Arabia and Iran at the OPEC conference revealed how easily frictions could arise among

OPEC members and how fragile the Organization could potentially become.

Indeed, during the mid-1970s the OPEC price policy was not always homogeneous: Saudi Arabia, on a longer-term perspective, advocated a prolongation of the price freeze which started in 1975 whereas most of the other countries favoured oil price increases to maintain their real purchasing power in front of their trading partners' mounting inflation. It was not until the end of 1978 that Iran, pressed by the USA, followed the Saudi Arabian policy of price restraint and OPEC succeeded in planning a longer-term pricing policy.

1.3.2   The second oil shock

OPEC's intentions notwithstanding, the overthrow of the Shah in Iran, in February 1979, fuelled a great uncertainty in the oil market: the spot price started to rise as importers were induced to pile their stocks. Consequently, many OPEC members pressed for a rise of the official price and were actually allowed to impose price premia. The situation collapsed in the last quarter of 1979 when Iran banned oil sales to US companies in response to the US economic embargo imposed to induce the release of US hostages. By November 1979 the oil spot price has risen from the official ceiling of $23.5 to over $40 per barrel and it remained high for the whole of 1980.

The structural change of the world energy market initiated by the first oil shock was thereby accelerated. Oil-importing countries severely cut their OPEC oil demand: between 1979 and 1982 the latter diminished by 12 million barrels per day; it is estimated (Brown, 1991) that 33 per cent of the drop in energy consumption was made possible by conservation measures and the economic recession, 25 per cent was ascribable to the increase of non-OPEC supply and 21 per cent to stock depletion by oil companies.

1.3.3   The oil market in the 1980s and the third oil price shock

During the first half of the 1980s the oil market regained competitiveness as oil companies, given the falling trend of consumption and the availability of non-OPEC oil, decided to move from long-term contracts to spot trading. By the end of 1983 the spot market was handling at least 40 per cent of the internationally traded oil while regular commodity exchanges facilitated the deals. Moreover, at the beginning of 1981, the USA had finally completed the abolition of oil price controls and their oil demand was again affecting the world oil market. Under these pressures the market price started to fall inducing non-OPEC producers, particularly the UK, to follow such a trend in order to increase their market share relative to OPEC. The latter's attempts to control its official price by limiting production were continuously threatened and finally failed because of internal conflicts (Iran–Iraqi war) and frictions (Saudi Arabia–Iran). These interior disagreements, coupled with the falling trend of the market price and the exports decline, determined continuous violations of the production quotas by non-Saudi members. Eventually, in December 1985, the OPEC conference decided to shift the priority from price defence to market share defence. The OPEC share of the world oil production rose from 29.5 per cent in the first half of 1985, to 32.6 per cent in the first half of 1986; this determined a considerable excess supply and caused a drastic fall of the oil price to less than $10 per barrel. Towards the end of 1986 OPEC decisions to reintroduce production quotas increased the price somewhat: the official OPEC price was set at $18 per barrel.

The most recent oil price upsurge was provoked by Iraq's invasion of Kuwait on 2 August 1990. This time the rise of the oil price was short lasting and fell back to its pre-crisis level during 1991 as other OPEC members decided to increase their production to sustain supply.

The policy followed by the Organization during this last emergency exemplifies how much its role has changed. OPEC now appears to have a limited ability to affect the international oil price (only 30 per cent of OPEC sales are made at the official price, OPEC exports cover 40 per cent of world oil demand, oil makes up nearly 50 per cent of world total energy supply), despite the fact that its members are the only oil producing countries, with the exception of Norway, which have control on spare capacity.

1.4   THE RELATIONSHIP BETWEEN OIL AND NON-OIL COMMODITY PRICES

The extent to which developments in the oil market have affected developments in non-oil primary commodities is a question which does not find a straightforward answer as the oil shock impacts are difficult to disentangle from those generated by the conditions of the overall world economy at those times. In what follows we intend to make some initial observations about this topic leaving further investigation to Chapter 3.

Figure 1.6 shows price indices for four broad groups of non-oil commodities: food, beverages, agricultural non-food raw materials and metals–minerals between 1958–1992.

Analogously to the oil market, which tightened before the 16 October 1973 OPEC decision, the prices of all groups of commodities also started to rise before the oil jump. These price increases were caused by several factors: first, the rapid

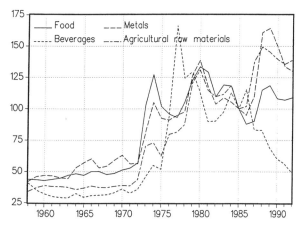

Figure 1.6   Non-oil primary commodity price indices

post-war expansion which, by the end of the 1960s, had generated severe tensions in the commodity markets as supply started being inadequate for the exploding demand; second, the early 1970s' monetary disorder which started with President Nixon's decision concerning dollar inconvertibility and proceeded to determine the end of the Bretton Woods international monetary system. The consequent uncertainty surrounding the purchasing power of the dollar, the diffused financial confusion and the exceptionally low real interest rates all contributed to create extraordinary high speculative and precautionary demands for raw materials.

During 1974, non-oil commodity prices rose again following some panic purchases, especially from Japan, although this oil-induced effect was short lasting given the looming recession of the industrialized countries. Apart from this largely speculative repercussion, a direct effect of the oil price shocks was probably to increase the marginal production cost of non-oil commodities; certainly higher oil prices imposed an upward pressure on the price of petroleum-based synthetic substitutes of natural raw materials. Subsequent to the first oil shock, non-oil commodities peaked again during the second oil shock then dropped in 1985 and, again, at the end of the 1980s.[7]

Granger-causality tests performed between oil and non-oil primary commodity prices confirm that the former Granger-cause the latter but not vice-versa;[8] this initial result, simply based on a bi-variate analysis, will be re-examined in Section 1.6 below and in Chapter 4. A positive effect of the oil price on non-oil commodity prices is, however, a common result in estimated non-oil primary price equations.[9]

1.5 THE FINANCIAL MARKETS IN THE AFTERMATH OF THE OIL SHOCKS

The abrupt rise of the price of oil in the early 1970s, together with the heavy external dependency of most Western economies on oil supply, caused a sharp shift in the shares of the world trade value. From 1973 to 1980, as shown in

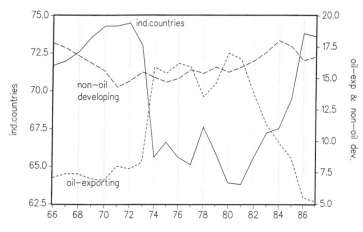

Figure 1.7   Industrialized countries: imports by origin

Figures 1.7 and 1.8 the value of both industrialized and non-oil developing country imports coming from oil-exporting countries rose considerably at the expense of the industrialized country export share: the immediate effect was a huge redistribution of the world wealth from the developed area to the oil-exporting one. The need to manage such a massive flow of resources became clear and gave rise to the so-called 're-

Figure 1.8   Non-oil developing countries: imports by origin

cycling' of oil surpluses in order to direct the latter back to the oil-importing countries to sustain their demand.

The data on capital trade reported in Table 1.3 give an idea of the exceptional capital exports that oil-exporting countries realized during 1974–78: on average they exported 36 current billion dollars per year against an annual average of 12 billion dollars exported by the developed economies during the previous boom in 1967–73. Most of these excess savings were transferred to non-oil developing countries through the intermediations of Western private banks. Among developing countries the major absorbers of such flows of capitals were the high and middle income developing economies; on the contrary low-income countries sustained their growing need of capitals by expanding aid flows (OECD, 1983; Table 1.4).

Indeed, during the 1970s, non-oil developing countries accumulated a mounting external debt. The latter, however, did not generate serious problems until the end of the decade: from 1973 to 1980 the debt/export ratio of most debtor countries remained constant and in some cases even improved: for non-oil-exporting LDC the debt/export ratio decreased from 115.4 in 1973 to 112.9 in 1980 (Sachs, 1989); moreover, from 1967–73 to 1974–78 the percentage of investments in GDP increased in all developing market economies (Table 1.3), contrary to was happening in the developed world. Indeed the macroeconomic situation was favouring debtors: inflation was eroding the real value of debt while debtor countries exports were rising at a pace higher than the interest rate which continued to remain at low levels for the whole decade.

The advent of the second oil shock drastically altered this happy situation. Western countries enforced restrictive policies to control the inflationary pressure and the economic recession that followed induced:

1. a severe reduction of the developing countries export earnings further worsened by a fall of commodity prices: between 1975–80 and 1981–85 the average annual percentage change

Table 1.3 Capital formation, domestic savings and international capital transfers

	Gross capital formation % GDP			Domestic savings % GDP (annual averages)			Capital imports (−)* Exports (+) % GDP			Capital imports (−)* Exports (+) Current US $ billion (annual averages)		
	60–66	67–73	74–88	60–66	67–73	74–88	60–66	67–73	74–78	60–66	67–73	74–78
World market economies	21.3	22.5	22.9	21.5	22.7	22.8	–	–	–	–	–	–
Developed market ec.	22.0	23.0	22.4	22.6	23.5	22.2	0.6	0.5	−0.2	7	12	−6
Major industrial	21.4	22.5	21.9	22.2	23.2	22.2	0.8	0.7	0.3	9	14	8
Other industrial	26.4	26.1	24.3	26.0	26.8	23.9	−0.4	0.7	−0.4	–	1	−1
Other developed	24.9	26.8	25.0	22.4	22.8	20.6	−2.5	−3.0	−4.4	−1	−4	−14
Developing market ec.	18.0	19.6	25.1	16.4	18.2	25.6	−1.6	−1.4	0.5	−5	−6	–
Oil exp. LDC	16.7	20.6	27.6	20.2	24.8	42.1	2.5	4.2	14.5	–	2	36
Oil imp. LDC	18.2	19.3	24.0	15.7	16.9	19.4	−2.5	−2.4	−4.6	−5	−6	−36
High income	20.5	21.0	25.6	18.6	18.9	21.3	−1.9	−2.1	−4.3	−1	−4	−19
Middle income	16.6	19.0	24.4	13.2	15.3	18.3	−3.4	−3.7	−6.1	−1	−2	−10
Low income	16.0	16.5	19.5	13.2	14.4	15.5	−2.8	−2.1	−4.0	−1	−1	−7
Africa												
Oil exp. LDC	21.3	24.0	34.5	20.3	26.0	37.0	−1.0	2.0	2.5	–	–	1
Oil imp. LDC	14.4	16.4	21.1	10.9	13.0	12.7	−3.5	−3.4	−8.4	−1	−1	−8
Latin American, Carrib.												
Oil exp. LDC	20.4	26.0	31.3	26.9	27.6	35.6	6.5	1.6	4.3	–	–	1
Oil imp. LDC	20.4	20.7	25.3	19.0	19.0	22.2	−1.4	−1.7	−3.1	−1	−2	−12
Asia and Oceania												
Oil exp. LDC	12.4	16.5	23.9	15.9	22.7	45.7	3.5	6.2	21.8	–	2	35
Oil imp. LDC	17.3	18.8	23.4	14.0	15.9	18.1	−3.3	−2.9	−5.3	−2	−4	−16

* Gross capital formation less gross domestic savings
Country Groups:
Major Industrial Economies: Canada, France, FRG, Italy, Japan, United Kingdom, United States.
Other Industrial Economies: Austria, Belgium, Denmark, Finland, Luxembourg, Netherlands, Norway, Sweden, Switzerland.
Other Developed Economies: Australia, Greece, Iceland, Ireland, Malta, New Zealand, Portugal, Puerto Rico, South Africa, Spain.
African Oil Exporters: Algeria, Gabon, Libya, Nigeria.

Table 1.4 Total resource flows to different categories of developing
countries, 1981

	NIC	MIC	OPEC	LIC	TOT
Total Resource Flow					
in $ billion	32.9	27.7	0.8	25.4	86.8
Percentage Share	37.9	31.9	0.9	29.3	100.0
Official Development					
Assistance (ODA)					
in $ billion	0.8	10.2	0.3	16.8	28.1
Percentage Share	2.8	36.3	1.1	59.8	100.0
Non-concessional					
in $ billion	32.1	17.5	0.5	8.6	58.7
Percentage Share	54.7	29.8	0.8	14.7	100.0
Bank lending (%)	88.9	22.7	–9.9	–1.7	100.0
Export credits (%)	34.9	29.8	8.5	26.8	100.0
Direct Invest. (%)	44.4	27.4	2.1	26.0	100.0
Multilateral (%)	34.5	47.0	0.9	17.6	100.0

Country Groups:
Low Income Countries (LIC) with GNP per capital below 600 $ in 1980;
Middle Income Countries (MIC) with GNP per capital above 600 $ in
1980;
Newly Industrialized Countries (NIC): Argentina, Brazil, Greece,
Hong Kong, Republic of Korea, Mexico, Portugal, Singapore, Spain,
Taiwan, Yugoslavia, OPEC members less Indonesia (included in LIC)
and Nigeria (included in MIC).
Source: OECD (1983)

of the export value of developing countries dropped from
20.5 per cent to –4.2 per cent (IMF, 1988);
2. a contemporaneous sudden rise of the real interest rate (see
   Figure 1.9). As the rate of growth of export earnings fell
   behind the interest rate indebted countries faced interest
   and principal payment problems: the prospects of a
   widespread default on foreign debt loomed and the
   situation collapsed in 1982 with a de facto moratorium on
   debt service by Mexico.

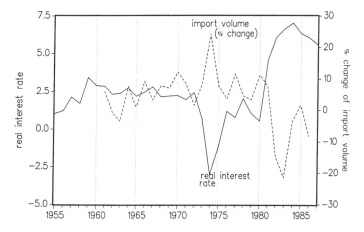

Figure 1.9   Real interest rate and highly indebted countries import volume

The early eighties debt crisis and the burdensome and pervasive effects that it caused worldwide well exemplify the relevance of the financial market in handling and carrying impulses and feedbacks through the system.

1.6   OECD ACTIVITY AND PRIMARY COMMODITY PRICES: A VECTOR AUTOREGRESSION ANALYSIS

As a preliminary statistical test on the links between primary commodity prices and the economic performance of the industrialized countries and as a useful material for the fully developed model we intend to build we perform Granger non-causality tests and cointegration analysis on vector autoregressions.

On account of the preceding discussion we consider a three-variable system where each variable may be thought of as representing a market: the OECD rate of unemployment summarizes the status of the OECD economy, the primary commodity price index, alternatively defined as total primary commodity-, non-oil primary commodity- or oil price-index, summarizes the primary commodity market and the real rate of interest represents the financial market.

The VAR system is the following:

$$y_t = \sum_{i=1}^{3} \mu_i y_{t-i} + v_t, v_t \sim IN(0, \Omega) \tag{1.1}$$

where $y' = [(pci - p), U, R]$ is the three-variable vector formed by a primary commodity price index, generally indicated by pci, in real terms,[10] the rate of OECD unemployment U and the real interest rate R.[11]

If the data in y_t are integrated of order 1, as we verify using univariate unit-root tests reported in Table 1.5,[12] a useful re-formulation of the VAR is to the error correction form (Doornik and Hendry, 1994) which permits us to separate the short-run from the long-run:

$$\Delta y_t = \sum_{i=1}^{2} \gamma_i \Delta y_{t-i} + P_0 y_{t-1} + v_t, v_t \sim IN(0, \Omega) \tag{1.2}$$

Notice that since y is I(1), Δy_t is I(0) and, for the system to be balanced, $P_0 y_{t-1}$ must also be I(0); this implies that the cointegrated vectors of the long-run solution, in other words the rank of the matrix P_0, can be at maximum two. We leave cointegration analysis to Section 1.6.2 and discuss, in this Section, the short-run properties of the model using multivariate Granger tests.

In equation (1.2) Granger non-causality tests are performed by testing the restriction that a set of $\gamma_i = 0$. For example, in the primary commodity price equation the tested restrictions are that the coefficients of the rate of unemployment and, alternatively, of the rate of interest, are not statistically different from zero; likewise for the other two equations.

This type of analysis, extensively used since the work of Sims (1972), provides an answer to the following question: 'How informative is a variable X in predicting those changes in a variable Y which are not already explained by past values of Y itself and of other observable variables?[13]

Since the variance of the relevant series increased dramatically within the period 1958–88, as we saw in the previous

Table 1.5   Unit root tests 1958–88

Results from estimating regressions of the form:

$$\Delta y_t = c + \alpha t + \beta y_{t-1} + \sum_{i=1}^{p} \eta_i \Delta y_{t-i}$$ where the lag length P is chosen in order to whiten the residuals.

R	DF	–0.68	ΔR	ADF	–6.83**
i_s	ADF c,t	–2.91	Δi_s	DF	–4.96**
i_l	ADF c,t	–2.56	Δi_l	DF	–3.83**
U	ADF c,t	–2.09	ΔU	DF	–4.04**
p_c	ADF c,t	–1.82	Δp_c	DF	–4.27**
p_n	ADF	1.68	Δp_n	ADF	–5.75**
p_o	DF	0.89	Δp_o	DF	–4.65**
$pc - p$	DF c	–1.58	$\Delta(pc - p)$	DF	–4.89**
$pn - p$	ADF	0.68	$\Delta(pn - p)$	ADF	–7.82**
$po - p$	DF c	–1.11	$\Delta(po - p)$	ADF	–5.26**
y	DF	–2.66	Δyc	DF	–3.72**

Note: Variables are defined as follows (see also data appendix):
p_c = log of total commodity price index in OECD currency
p_n = log of non-oil commodity price in OECD currency
p_o = log of oil price in OECD currency
p = log of OECD GDP deflator
i_s = short term interest rate
i_l = long term interest rate
R = real long term interest rate
U = rate of OECD unemployment
y = log of OECD GDP
For any variable x, $\Delta x = x_t - x_{t-1}$. When $\eta_i = 0$ the unit-root test is a Dickey-Fuller test (DF), otherwise it is an Augmented DF test (ADF). The letters c and t next to the test indicate whether a constant and a time trend are included or not.
** significance at 99%, * significance at 95%.

---

section, the analysis is also performed separately for the two sub-periods 1958–72 and 1973–88.

1.6.1   Multivariate Granger-causality tests

Table 1.6 reports the X^2 statistic testing the significance of the primary commodity price index in the rate of unemployment

Table 1.6 $X^2(2)$ test for the significance of the primary commodity price index in the rate of unemployment equation

Primary commodity price used:	1958–88	1958–72	1973–88
$pc - p$	38.855**	8.0733*	19.187**
$pn - p$	12.531**	5.979*	10.486**
$po - p$	25.294**	0.4098	16.030**

Note: Three variable system $y' = [(pci - p), U, R]$.
All variables in first differences, two lags on each variable.
** significance at 99%, * significance at 95%.
Variable definition in Table 1.5.

equation. On the whole period the significance is unambiguous and reaches a 99 per cent level of significance regardless of the primary commodity price index used. However, when separating the pre- from the post-1973 period, the same level of significance holds for the post-oil-shock sub-period only whereas from 1958 to 1972 the statistical significance drops to 95 per cent for the total and the non-oil primary price indices and disappears for the oil price index.

As far as the significance of the OECD unemployment rate in the primary commodity price equation is concerned, the $X^2(2)$ results reported in Table 1.7 are clear: whatever the primary commodity price variable used, the rate of OECD unemployment does not carry any statistically relevant information in the primary commodity price equation; in fact the level of significance is higher in the non-oil primary price equation but never reaches 90 per cent.

This result is quite plausible for the price of oil whose developments have been to a great extent independent of the OECD economic activity[14] but is surprising for the non-oil primary commodity price index which we expected to respond to the OECD economic activity.

Table 1.7 $X^2(2)$ test for the significance of the rate of unemployment in the primary commodity price equation

Primary commodity price used	1958–88	1958–72	1973–88
$pc - p$	1.2109	3.7552	0.3726
$pn - p$	3.4473	3.502	3.4793
$po - p$	0.8401	1.6023	0.5463

Note: Three variable system $y' = [(pci - p), U, R]$.
All variables in first differences, two lags on each variable.
** significance at 99%, * significance at 95%.
Variable definition in Table 1.5.

It may be that the unemployment rate is not a suitable indicator of the OECD demand and we replace it with OECD GDP. Also in this case (Table 1.8) the evidence of a Granger-causality running from OECD economic activity to primary commodity prices remains feeble, although in the total primary commodity price equation the restrictions are now rejected at 90 per cent.

As a second test we investigated the possibility that the short-run relationship we are looking at is in fact between the OECD economic activity and the *nominal* price of primary commodities, whereas the real price is pinned down only in the long run.[15] The vector is then modified to comprise, in the short run, the nominal price of primary commodities, the OECD unemployment rate and the short-term nominal interest rate $y' = (pci, U, i_s)$.

Results are reported in Table 1.9: between 1958 and 1988 the OECD rate of unemployment now carries significant information in all primary commodity price equations; sub-period inspection indicates that such a link becomes significant only after 1972 and is particularly robust for the non-oil component of primary commodities.

Table 1.8 $X^2(2)$ test for the significance of OECD GDP in the primary commodity price equation

Primary commodity price used	1958–88	1958–72	1973–88
$pc - p$	5.0130ˆ	0.4403	2.6332
$pn - p$	1.2121	2.7233	0.6870
$po - p$	1.9503	1.2724	2.5265

Note: Three variable system $y' = [(pci - p), y, R]$.
All variables in first differences, two lags on each variable.
** significance at 99%, * significance at 95%, ˆ significance at 90%.
Variable definition in Table 1.5.

Table 1.9 $X^2(2)$ test for the significance of OECD rate of unemployment in the primary commodity price equation

Primary commodity price used	1958–88	1958–72	1973–88
pc	9.1150*	1.3727	6.6876*
pn	14.6500**	0.2820	11.977**
po	6.0509*	4.1889	2.1203

Note: Three variable system $y' = [pci, U, i_s]$.
All variables in first differences, two lags on each variable.
** significance at 99%, * significance at 95%, ˆ significance at 90%.
Variable definition in Table 1.5.

As far as the real interest rate is concerned, its significance for the rate of unemployment (Table 1.10) is evident only in the first sub-period and when the system comprises either the total- or the non-oil primary commodity price index. In the second sub-period the reverse causality is present, that is,

Table 1.10 $X^2(2)$ test for the significance of the real interest rate in the rate of unemployment equation

Primary commodity price used:	1958–88	1958–72	1973–88
$pc - p$	1.1642	7.2454*	1.2141
$pn - p$	0.1548	8.3881*	2.0694
$po - p$	2.9008	3.6380	3.6188

Note: Three variable system $y' = [(pci - p), U, R]$.
All variables in first differences, two lags on each variable.
** significance at 99%, * significance at 95%.
Variable definition in Table 1.5.

Table 1.11 $X^2(2)$ test for the significance of rate of unemployment in the real interest rate equation

Primary commodity price used:	1958–88	1958–72	1973–88
$pc - p$	7.7815	1.1082	8.1235*
$pn - p$	15.8280**	2.9664	16.6580**
$po - p$	7.6585*	1.9637	7.4768*

Note: Three variable system $y' = [(pci - p), U, R]$.
All variables in first differences, two lags on each variable.
** significance at 99%, * significance at 95%.
Variable definition in Table 1.5.

the rate of unemployment is significant for the real interest rate (Table 1.11); again the significance is robust especially in the presence of non-oil commodity prices.

On the contrary, there is no manifest significance of either the real interest rate in the commodity price equation or the primary commodity price in the real interest rate equation.

Table 1.12 $X^2(2)$ test for the significance of the short-term nominal interest rate in the primary commodity price equation

Primary commodity price used	1958–88	1958–72	1973–88
pc	31.8720**	0.61239	24.0450**
pn	8.9744*	3.3544	8.5039*
po	32.0440**	2.6057	18.6190**

Note: Three variable system $y' = [pci, U, i_s]$.
All variables in first differences, two lags on each variable.
** significance at 99%, * significance at 95%.
Variable definition in Table 1.5.

This last result is re-examined using the vector $y' = (pci, U, i_s)$. In this case the causality running from the nominal rate of interest to the nominal price of primary commodities is well-defined on the whole period and for all price indices (Table 1.12); however sub-period tests indicate that the significance comes exclusively from the second sub-period and that the level of significance is higher for the oil price. This could imply that the 'financial' information conveyed by the rate of interest is relatively more important for the oil component of the commodity price, whereas the 'real activity indicator', captured by the rate of unemployment is relatively more important for the non-oil component. On the other hand the result according to which primary prices do not Granger-cause the rate of interest remains even when considering nominal variables (Table 1.13).

We can summarize the main findings of the above short-run analysis in the following points:

1. Real primary commodity prices are important in forecasting the OECD rate of unemployment, given the real interest rate.

Table 1.13 $X^2(2)$ test for the significance of the primary commodity
price index in the short-term nominal interest rate equation

Primary commodity price used	1958–88	1958–72	1973–88
pc	1.0837	3.0390	0.0788
pn	1.6216	4.8295ˆ	0.0274
po	2.7217	1.2047	1.0479

Note: Three variable system $y' = [\,pci, U, i_s]$.
All variables in first differences, two lags on each variable.
** significance at 99%, * significance at 95% ˆsignificance at 90%.
Variable definition in Table 1.5.

2. The OECD rate of unemployment is important in forecasting nominal primary commodity prices, given the nominal short-term interest rate.
3. Between 1958 and 1972 the real interest rate Granger-causes the rate of unemployment, given real primary commodity prices; the reverse causality holds specially between 1973 and 1988.
4. The short-term nominal interest rate is important in forecasting nominal primary commodity prices, given the OECD rate of unemployment but nominal primary commodity prices do not Granger-cause the short-term nominal interest rate.
5. Neither direct or reverse causality is present between real primary commodity prices and the real rate of interest.

In an important survey Labys and Maizels (1993) use bivariate Granger-causality tests to investigate the link between commodity prices and industrial activity for six major OECD countries from 1957 to 1986 using quarterly data. Their results confirm that both the total commodity price and the energy price Granger-cause GDP except for the USA. Using industrial production the relation is usually stronger but only in a few cases (Germany, Italy) presents feedbacks.[16]

1.6.2 Cointegration analysis

In this Section some preliminary tests are performed in order to establish the existence or otherwise of a long-run relationship between OECD economic activity, primary commodity prices and the real interest rate.

The long-run properties of the system are captured by the matrix P_0 which is usually parted into two matrices: $P_0 = \alpha \cdot \beta'$. The matrix β encloses the ρ cointegrating vectors, that is the coefficients of the error correction mechanisms (ECM); the matrix α contains the weights or 'loadings' with which each cointegrating vector or ECM enters each equation of the system.

We assume that in the long-run all variables are determined in real terms and consider four alternative VAR systems which differ according to the primary price index introduced: similarly to the previous analysis the primary price index is alternatively defined as the total primary commodity price index, the non-oil commodity price index or the oil price index; in the last VAR oil and non-oil commodity price indices are simultaneously present. Each VAR also includes the OECD rate of unemployment and the real interest rate; the time trend is also allowed to enter the long-run and the constant is defined as unrestricted.

Therefore, in the first three cases, the cointegration space is spanned by three I(1) variables and a linear trend and in the last case it is spanned by four I(1) variables and again a time trend. It follows that the maximum number of cointegrating vectors, i.e. the maximum rank of the matrix P_0 is two for the three basic models and three for the extended model. Notice, finally, that in order to support the possibility of a two-way relationship between the OECD economy and the primary commodity market we would like to find at least two cointegrating vectors.

Although all variables entering the VAR are I(1), as the DF and the ADF tests of Table 1.5 prove, in the period under consideration most of the variables experience diverse 'structural breaks' which may be easily confounded with authentic unit roots.[17] Although a few preliminary tests confirm the presence of unit roots even when structural breaks are controlled for, it is necessary, once these breaks have been identified, to control for them also in the cointegration analysis using unrestricted step-dummies.[18]

The identification of structural breaks in time series (Banerjee and Urga, 1995, Banerjee *et al.*, 1992 and Perron 1989) is very difficult unless the break is easily related to a clear economic event. The step dummies included in the following cointegration analysis correspond to the breaks identified by the 1-step ahead Chow test on the recursive estimates of the VAR systems and are easily related to the economic shocks.[19]

Table 1.14 reports the Johansen (1988) cointegration tests for the four VAR models we considered. Both the trace and maximum eigenvalue statistics are provided in order to determine the rank ρ of the matrix P_0, that is, the number of cointegrated vectors; the two statistics have the same null hypothesis but a different alternative hypothesis, as shown in the table. Both the trace and the maximum eigenvalue agree on the existence of two cointegrated vectors in the model comprising the total primary commodity price index and in the model including the oil price; on the other hand only one cointegrated vector is present in the model using the non-oil commodity price index. Finally, when both the oil and the non-oil price indices are simultaneously included three cointegrated vectors are possibly present.

The last two tables report the estimated cointegrated vectors; Table 1.15 presents the vectors of the three basic models and Table 1.16 those of the extended model. In presence of more than one cointegrated vector we report the vectors obtained by normalizing the highest as well as the second highest and in the extended model even the third highest eigenvalues (the eigenvalues are shown in Table 1.14).

Table 1.14 Johansen cointegration tests

Primary commodity price in VAR model

Null Hypoth	Trace Altern.	Max λ Alternative	pc – p Trace	Max λ	Eigenv.	pn – p Trace	Max λ	Eigenv.	po – p Trace	Max λ	Eigenv.	Critical values Trace 95%	Max λ 95%
ρ = 0	ρ > = 1	ρ = 1	90.73**	56.68**	0.839319	51.26**	31.96**	0.643341	72.07**	40.54**	0.729533	42.4	25.5
ρ < = 1	ρ > = 2	ρ = 2	34.06**	27.53**	0.588577	19.30	17.29	0.427553	31.53**	24.96**	0.553029	25.3	19.0
ρ < = 2	ρ > = 3	ρ = 3	5.892	5.892	0.189752	2.005	2.005	0.0626167	6.572	6.572	0.191028	12.2	12.2

Primary commodity price in VAR model

pn – p, po – p

Null Hypoth	Trace Altern.	Max λ Alternative	Trace	Max λ	Eigenv.	Critical values Trace 95%	Max λ 95%
ρ = 0	ρ > = 1	ρ = 1	109.1**	47.89**	0.786635	63.0	31.5
ρ < = 1	ρ > = 2	ρ = 2	61.18**	33.31**	0.658547	42.4	25.5
ρ < = 2	ρ > = 3	ρ = 3	27.87*	21.19*	0.495175	25.3	19.0
ρ < = 3	ρ = 4	ρ = 4	6.684	6.684	0.193948	12.2	12.2

Note: **/* denote significance at 99/95% level of significance.

Moreover the vectors shown differ according to the endogenous variable used to normalize the eigenvalues.

When the normalization is with respect to U, a positive sign on the primary commodity price index would indicate that a rise in the price of primary commodities is associated with an increase of the OECD rate of unemployment; indeed a positive coefficient is present in four out of the five cases of Table 1.15. However, using the extended model, it turns out that the impact on the unemployment rate differs according to the component of primary price index (Table 1.16): the price of oil shows a positive sign whereas the non-oil price shows a negative sign.

When the normalization is with respect to the primary commodity price, a negative sign on the coefficient of the rate of unemployment would denote that a decline of the OECD economic activity, that is a rise of the unemployment rate, depresses the price of primary commodities. However in Table 1.15 this happens only in one case out of five (in the model comprising the total primary commodity price). In Table 1.16 a negative sign of the rate of unemployment is always present when the normalization is with respect to $pn - p$ whereas the rate of unemployment always shows a positive sign when the normalization is with respect to the price of oil. The unexpected sign on the rate of unemployment when the normalization is with respect to the price of oil, both in the basic and in the extended model, corroborates the idea that the price of oil is probably exogenous to the model.

Finally, when the normalization is with respect to R the signs on both the rate of unemployment and the primary commodity price indices are not well defined.

We may conclude that in the first basic model, using $pc - p$, two cointegrated vectors with reasonable signs are those of columns two and three; in the second basic model, using $pn - p$, the only sensible cointegrated vector appears that of column one; in the third basic model two plausible cointegrated vectors could be found among those of columns one, two, five and six. Finally, in the extended model the three cointegrated

Table 1.15 Estimated cointegrated vectors in Johansen estimation (normalized)

Primary commodity price in VAR model
$pc - p$

| | Normalized with respect to: | | | | | |
| | U | | $pc - p$ | | R | |
	(1)	(2)	(1)	(2)	(1)	(2)
U	−1.00	−1.00	−121.20	24.74	−0.2496	3.585
$pc - p$	−0.0082	0.04042	−1.00	−1.00	−0.00206	−0.1449
R	−4.006	0.279	−485.60	−6.901	−1.00	−1.00
t	−0.0008	0.00195	−0.099	−0.048	−0.0002	−0.00698

Primary Commodity Price in VAR Model
$pn - p$

| | Normalized with respect to: | | |
| | U | $pn - p$ | R |
	(1)	(1)	(1)
U	−1.00	10.84	−0.6782
$pn - p$	0.09223	−1.00	0.06255
R	−1.474	15.99	−1.00
t	0.0005	−0.0057	0.00036

Primary Commodity Price in VAR Model
$po - p$

| | Normalized with respect to: | | | | | |
| | U | | $po - p$ | | R | |
	(1)	(2)	(1)	(2)	(1)	(2)
U	−1.00	−1.00	60.73	51.82	−1.032	2.490
$po - p$	0.01647	0.0193	−1.00	−1.00	0.0170	−0.04805
R	−0.9688	0.4016	58.83	−20.81	−1.00	−1.00
t	0.00034	0.00024	−0.02074	−0.02161	0.00035	−0.001038

Note: (1)/(2) denote whether the normalization is with respect to the highest/second highest eigenvalue

Table 1.16 Estimated cointegrated vectors in Johansen procedure (normalized)

Primary Commodity Price in VAR Model
pn − p, po − p

Normalization with respect to:

	U			pn − p			po − p			R		
	(1)	(2)	(3)	(1)	(2)	(3)	(1)	(2)	(3)	(1)	(2)	(3)
U	−1.00	−1.00	−1.00	−14.67	−215.3	−4.018	43.48	43.48	16.11	−1.0016	2.628	1.829
pn − p	−0.0682	−0.0046	−0.2489	−1.00	−1.00	−1.00	2.965	0.2036	4.010	−0.0692	0.0122	0.4551
po − p	0.0230	0.02281	0.06207	0.3373	4.911	0.2494	−1.00	−1.00	−1.00	0.0233	−0.05993	−0.1135
R	−0.9847	0.3806	0.5469	−14.44	81.95	2.197	42.82	−16.69	−8.811	−1.00	−1.00	−1.00
t	−0.00079	0.00062	−0.00269	−0.01159	0.1341	−0.01079	0.03435	−0.02731	0.04328	−0.0008	−0.00164	0.00491

Note: (1)/(2)/(3) denote whether the normalization is with respect to the highest/second highest/third highest eigenvalue vectors could be found among the vectors normalized with respect to U, $pn - p$ and R.

On the whole this initial analysis of cointegration corroborates the hypothesis of a two-way relationship between primary commodity prices and the OECD rate of unemployment conditional on the inclusion, either in an aggregated price index or as a separate variable, of the price of oil although the findings seem to confirm that the latter is probably exogenous to the model. Moreover, the diverse impact of oil and non-oil components of the primary price index on the rate of unemployment calls for a separate consideration of the two prices in the empirical analysis.

The further question of identifying the unique cointegrating relations is not pursued here and left to a subsequent study.

1.7 LAYOUT OF THE BOOK

Chapter 2 describes the analytical model and the theory behind it; to facilitate the reading, detailed algebra is separately presented in Chapter 3. In Chapter 2, following a description of the functioning of each market, we discuss the theoretical working of the overall model. In particular the long-run properties are described using a novel diagrammatical approach which supports the algebraical analysis; in addition the structure of the model allows us to examine the factors generating short-run nominal inertia and to investigate the degree of hysteresis of the rate of unemployment. Here the role played by primary commodity prices as well as the effects of the world financial market are explicitly derived.

Chapter 4 confronts the evidence. The model is estimated on historical data from 1958 to 1988 and is subsequently used to obtain evidence on the main theoretical aspects outlined in Chapter 2. These concern the forces behind the low-frequency movements of the endogenous variables, the quantitative appraisal of hysteresis of the OECD unemployment rate and the effects of the external markets, the factors affecting price forecasting errors and inflation growth.

The estimated model is then dynamically simulated both on historical data and on the assumption of a twofold oil price shock. By studying the resulting dynamic multipliers some important aspects about the working of the propagation mechanism are uncovered: in particular the role of the different markets in transmitting the shock as well as the effects of short-run demand factors can be featured quite clearly.

The final chapter recounts the main phases of the research and assesses the key theoretical and empirical findings.

APPENDIX TO CHAPTER 1: IMPORT UNIT VALUE AND PRIMARY COMMODITY PRICE INDEX

Define:

p_m = log price of total imports,

p_c = log price of primary commodity imports,

p_g = log price of gross output,

p_{ma} = log price of manufactured goods,

p = log price of value added,

α_1 = share of primary commodities in total imports,

α_2 = share of primary commodities in gross output,

s = share of imports in value added.

The following definitions hold:

i) $p_m = \alpha_1 p_c + (1 - \alpha_1) p_{ma}$
ii) $p_g = \alpha_2 p_c + (1 - \alpha_2) p_{ma}$
iii) $p = (1 + s) p_g - s p_m$

In order to obtain a relationship between $(p_m - p)$ and $(p_c - p)$, substitute i) and ii) into iii):

iv) $p = (1 + s) \alpha_2 p_c + (1 + s) (1 - \alpha_2) p_{ma} - s \alpha_1 p_c$
$- s (1 - \alpha_1) p_{ma}$

Subtract iv) from i) and from ii) to obtain:

v) $p_m - p = (1 + s)(\alpha_1 - \alpha_2)[p_c - p_{ma}]$
vi) $p_c - p = [(1 - \alpha_2) + s(\alpha_1 - \alpha_2)][p_c - p_{ma}]$

Hence:

vii) $p_m - p = \dfrac{(1+s)(\alpha_1 - \alpha_2)}{(1 - \alpha_2) + s(\alpha_1 - \alpha_2)}(p_c - p)$

There are two cases for which $(p_m - p)$ is directly proportional to $(p_c - p)$.

a) $\alpha_1 > \alpha_2$
b) $\alpha_1 < \alpha_2$ and $(1 - \alpha_2) < s(\alpha_2 - \alpha_1)$,
   i.e. $s > (1 - \alpha_2)/(\alpha_2 - \alpha_1)$.

Note that this simple result no longer holds if gross output also includes domestic services. If the price of domestic services, however, does not fluctuate too much compared to that of manufactured goods, then there is still a linear relationship between real import prices and real commodity prices.

2 The Outline of the Theory

The troublesome years that followed the first oil shock witnessed unusual changes in many important macroeconomic variables. The facts recollected in the previous chapter indicate that these sharp variations can be related and somehow traced back to the developments of three pivotal variables: the OECD rate of unemployment, the primary commodity price index and the real rate of interest.

In this chapter, we build from the theoretical determination of these three variables in order to set up a representative macroeconomic model which can account for the facts in a sufficiently detailed manner and which makes explicit the various links connecting the relevant macroeconomic variables. The objective of this chapter is to present the basic elements of the model in order to allow an understanding of its overall functioning. Analytical details are postponed to Chapter 3; the latter, however, is not indispensable for the comprehension of the empirical part of the book for which the reading of the present chapter is sufficient.

The model can be usefully described as an interacting set of markets grouped into OECD markets, LDC markets and international markets. The latter are the financial and the primary commodity market and constitute the *traid d'union* between the OECD and the Southern region.

All nominal variables are assumed to be expressed in 'OECD currency', that is, the basket of currencies entering the bloc. The choice of using a common OECD currency rather than converting all indices to a dollar basis, rests essentially on practical reasons since this is the procedure adopted by the IMF from whose sources we collected most of the data used in the empirical work.[1]

This model has been initially conceived as an extension of the Layard–Nickell (1986) model; although successive elaborations have introduced further departures from the original framework it should still be interpreted in that spirit.

2.1 THE OECD PRODUCT MARKET

The OECD supply side is determined by the interplay of the product and the labour market. The product market is imperfectly competitive: firms, on the basis of their expectations on demand and wages, set the price of output and, given the production function, decide the level of employment.

The production function used throughout the book is a value added one on the assumption that gross output is a separate function of raw materials, on the one side, and value added, on the other.[2] Value added, or GDP, in turn, is determined by the use of capital and labour given the available technology. Short-run discrepancies between desired and available labour input are possible and are met by adjusting working hours; deviations of the latter from their trend are, therefore, an additional element in the production function. The level of output planned and produced by the firms satisfies aggregate demand as forecasted by the firms themselves; on this basis the level of employment can be derived by inverting the production function.

Expected aggregate demand and consequently production and employment depend on the price level that will prevail. Each firm, following the profit maximizing rationale, sets the price of output in order to cover the expected marginal variable costs plus a mark-up. The latter we take to be potentially subject to cyclical movements[3] approximated by two important variables: the rate of unemployment, which captures deviations of demand from trend, and the real interest rate which is the intertemporal price the firms look at whenever a comparison between today's profits and the expected future flow of revenues is necessary.[4]

Finally, the price equation results to be a function of a measure of trend productivity, of deviations of working hours from trend, of wage and price forecasting errors, of the rate of unemployment and of the real rate of interest.

The production function and the price mark-up equation, expressed in logarithms, are therefore specified as follows:[5]

$$y - k = c_1 + a_1(n - k) + d_1 k + e_1 a + n_1(h - \bar{h}) \qquad (2.1)$$

$$p - w = c_2 - a_2(y^e - l) + b_2 R - d_2 U + e_2(p - p^e)$$
$$\qquad - f_2(w - w^e) + m_2(h - \bar{h}) \qquad (2.2)$$

where y = log of GDP, y^e = log of expected GDP, n = log of employment, k = log of capital stock, a = log of technical progress index, h = log of working hours, $\bar{h}$ = log of trend working hours, p = log of output price, p^e = log of expected output price, w = log of wage w^e = log of expected wage, R = real interest rate, U = rate of unemployment.

The above equations, as well as the remaining ones in this chapter, are usually presented, for convenience, in their static form. In practice the presence of adjustment costs will introduce dynamics into the equations allowing both the dependent and the independent variables to appear with lags, the distribution of which is chosen empirically; the importance of dynamics is discussed in Section 2.9 below.

2.2   THE FUNCTIONING OF THE OECD LABOUR MARKET

It is well-known that the institutional structure of the labour market, which crucially affects the determination of the nominal wage, is quite heterogeneous among OECD countries. In North America and Britain competitiveness prevails, in Scandinavia and Austria unions are powerful and centralized and bargain with a national employers' federation, in Southern Europe unions are strong but decentralized by industry, in Japan the labour market is rather idiosyncratic with a level of unionization lower than in the USA, a medium degree of centralization but a high consensus and a good inter-union and inter-firm coordination (see for example Tarantelli, 1986 and Layard *et al.* 1991). In addition, the extent of government intervention and the role of welfare policies like benefit coverage, duration and amount are also highly differentiated and cluster the countries in different groups (Blank, 1993).

Diverse wage determination mechanisms are, therefore, likely to be contemporaneously present in the OECD system implying that the modelling of an OECD aggregated wage equation must be sufficiently general to comprehend the various features. Therefore three institutionally different labour markets are considered: one dominated by demand and supply, a second one driven by efficiency wage considerations and a final one characterized by the presence of insiders or groups of insiders organized in unions.

The detailed description of each case and the derivation of the associated wage equations is left to Chapter 3. Here we report and comment on the determinants of the final specification obtained by aggregating the separate equations.

$$w - p = c_3 + a_3(y^e - l) - b_3 R + d_{31} U_{-1} + d_{32} lnU - e_3(p - p^e)$$
$$+ f_3(w - w^e) + g_3 \chi(pc - p) + h_3 T$$
$$+ i_3 \frac{NC}{N} + l_3 y^e + m_3(h - \bar{h}) \qquad (2.3)$$

where $(y^e - l)$ is a measure of trend productivity, l is the log of the labour force, χ is the input share in gross output, pc is the index of total primary commodity prices, T is the tax rate given by the sum of employee and employer tax rates, NC/N is the number of industrial conflicts normalized to number of employees.

A few features of the above equation are worthwhile remarking:

1. As in standard real wage equations deflated by GDP deflator, a measure of the wedge is present; this enters via the tax rates borne by the firm and by the employee and via the relative import price index.

2. In addition to a measure of trend productivity, there is another trending variable in the form of expected demand which enters via the efficiency-wage model.
3. The rate of unemployment stems from the insider–outsider model and from the efficiency wage model; the former should entail a positive effect of the lagged rate of unemployment whereas the latter one introduces the logarithm of the rate of unemployment.
4. The presence of the real interest rate, whose coefficient is linked to that entering the price equation, depends on the relevance of the competitive model and of the insider-outsider one. As discussed in the next chapter, the presence of the real interest rate, usually neglected in the real wage equations,[6] is crucial in assessing the influence of the real interest rate on the rate of unemployment.
5. The relative importance of the union–insider dominated labour market is captured, in the empirical wage equation, by some indicator of union power which is usually a significant regressor in wage equations. A good measure of union power is the ratio of union to non-union mark-up (for example Layard and Nickell, 1986); however, since a complete series of the latter is not available at the OECD level, we use the number of industrial conflicts normalized to number of employees. This indicator is endogenized using a simple model.

2.3   INDUSTRIAL CONFLICTS

Figure 2.1 shows the development of industrial conflicts: a strife wave is clear between the late 1960s and the first half of the 1970s and, quite interestingly, the timing of this increase is closely related to that of inflation.[7] After that, almost in conjunction with the increasing rates of unemployment, industrial conflicts start declining.

Strikes are unjustifiable according to standard economic rationality: a halt reduces the total available product, hence strikes cannot be, ex-post, Pareto optimal. Hicks (1963) argues

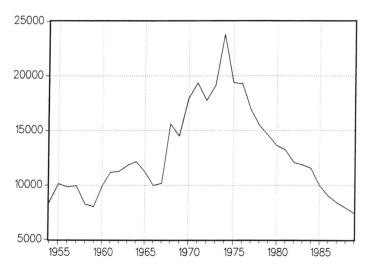

Figure 2.1 Number of industrial conflicts in the OECD

that adequate knowledge would always make settlements possible although unions would still be inclined to strike in order to sustain the credibility of their threats. Therefore Hicks assumes a standard rational behaviour for the firms but his approach is looser as far as the workers' conduct is concerned.

On the wave of the so-called 'Hicks' paradox' the economics of strikes succeeded in stimulating new research. Most theories explain conflicts by the interplay of unions and firms but, in order to be successful, must relax either the rationality assumption or the perfect information assumption. The well-known model by Ashenfelter and Johnson (1969), for example, does not assume rational behaviour on the part of the workers; strikes are explained by the interaction between the union's 'resistance curve' and the firm's conceivable wage increase. More recent bargaining theories of strikes restore ex-ante rationality by assuming asymmetric information (Kennan, 1986).

The model of strikes used below (Cristini, 1989) stems from the well-known concept of 'relative' wage which typically applies when different groups of workers interact. According to this view a divergence of the actual wage structure from the 'equilibrium' one is likely to produce discontent and strife among workers. Extending this idea to a more general case, strikes may be viewed as the results of tensions arising whenever the actual consumption wage deviates from the 'aspired' one by more than the cost of holding a strike. Industrial conflicts are therefore determined by those factors which open a gap between the desired and the actual real wage (variables affecting the wedge, for example) as well as by factors influencing the cost of the strike, measured by the potential earnings obtainable in case the strike is abandoned. Leaving details to the next chapter, the number of conflict equation looks as follows:

$$\frac{NC}{N} = c_4 - d_4 U + g_4 \chi (pc - p) + g_{41} \chi \Delta (pc - p) + h_4 T$$
$$+ d_{41} \Delta T \qquad (2.4)$$

2.4   THE WORKING OF THE OECD SUPPLY SIDE

In order to close the OECD supply side we include an important identity which links the OECD rate of unemployment to the logarithm of the labour force and employment:

$$U = l - n \qquad (2.5)$$

Finally, although it is not our intention to model labour supply, a simple behavioural equation is added in order to account for some of the feedbacks; labour force is linked to a time trend t and to the expected real wage:

$$l = c_5 + h_5 t + i_5 (w - p)^e \qquad (2.6)$$

Equations (2.1) to (2.6) then shape the OECD supply side. The essential features of its functioning are described by a simple and by now well-known diagram which sketches the price and wage equations in the $(w - p) - U$ space (Layard and Nickell,

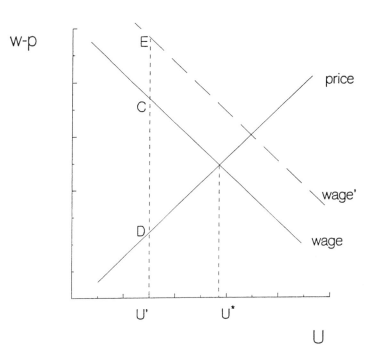

Figure 2.2 North equilibrium

1986; Layard *et al.*, 1991).[8] As illustrated in Figure 2.2, in the $U - (w - p)$ space the price equation is likely to be upward sloping (a rise in U lowers the expected marginal costs and may affect the mark-up) whereas the wage equation is downward sloping (a rise in U implies excess supply and also decreases unions' strength). Also observe that the intercepts of both lines depends also on price and wage forecasting errors: hence the gap existing between $(w - p)$ and $(p - w)$ is proportional to nominal forecasting errors while the rate of unemployment, which we obtain by solving the wage and the price equation, depends, *inter alia*, on such surprises. It is only when the latter are set to zero, that is, when expectations are fulfilled, that the rate of unemployment identifies the rate of unemployment consistent with no forecasting errors. Notice that the latter is a

NAIRU as long as price and wage surprises are associated with the rate of inflation;[9] however, as we shall discuss, it is a partial equilibrium NAIRU.

Using Figure 2.2 we can trace the impact of an exogenous shock according to this initial partial equilibrium system. Suppose that the North follows an expansionary policy in order to bring the rate of unemployment below U*. Depending on the relative inertia of wages and prices the real wage will set at a new point between C and D, thereby initiating a positive rate of inflation. In addition, the expansionary policy rises demand for primary commodities the price of which will rise determining a rightward shift of the wage line and thereby making inflation proportional to the segment ED rather than CD. If the expansion is 'once and for all' real money balance effects will take the system back to the original long-run equilibrium; alternatively the lower rate of unemployment can be preserved by trying to move the wage equation leftwards to point D.[10] A well-known way to achieve such an objective, for example, is by appreciating the OECD currency relative to the LDC currency; this policy, however, is detrimental for the LDC bloc and likely to involve large balance of payment deficits in the North.

The working of the OECD supply side just described is conditional on expected demand, on the real interest rate and, most importantly, on the price of primary commodities. An extended diagram, capable of illustrating these further links will be introduced after discussing the theoretical determination of these macroeconomic variables.

2.5   OECD AND LDC AGGREGATE DEMAND

Aggregate demand, for both OECD and LDC is a log-linear function of the usual national account components:

$$lnY = \alpha_C lnC + \alpha_I lnI + \alpha_G lnG + \alpha_X lnX - \alpha_M lnM \qquad (2.7)$$
$$lnY^* = \alpha_C lnC^* + \alpha_I lnI^* + \alpha_G lnG^* + \alpha_X lnX^*$$
$$- \alpha_M lnM^* \qquad (2.8)$$

where a star identifies LDC variables, C is consumption, I investments, G public expenditure, X exports and M imports and α's are the weights of the single components.

Each component is defined in a standard fashion. Private consumption depends on disposable income, real money balances, inflation and the real interest rate; private investments are a function of expected demand growth, as in the accelerator tradition, but may also depend on a number of other factors associated with the relative cost of internal versus external finance, in the more recent tradition of the asymmetric information approach.[11] Public expenditure, taxes and nominal money supply are assumed to be exogenous policy instruments;[12] exports depend on the rest of the world income and on competitiveness; likewise imports depend on national income and competitiveness.

By substituting the definitions of the various components and solving for Y, as presented in the next chapter, the OECD aggregate demand function looks as follows:

$$y = \frac{1}{\alpha}\left(c_6 + b_6R - e_6\Delta p + g_6(pc - p) + h_6y^* - i_6T + l_6(g - p)\right.$$
$$\left. + m_6(m - p) + n_6\Pi^e - p_6y_{-1}\right) \qquad (2.9)$$

where small letter indicates logarithms, α is the Keynesian multiplier, Δp is the rate of inflation, in terms of GDP deflator and Π^e is the log of the firms' expected real profits. An analogous expression can be derived for the LDC:

$$y^* = \frac{1}{\alpha^*}\left(c_7 + b_7R - e_7\Delta pc - g_7(pc - p) + h_7y - i_7T^*\right.$$
$$\left. + l_7(g - p)^* + m_7(m - p) + n_7\Pi^{*e} - p_7y^*_{-1}\right) \qquad (2.10)$$

2.6 CURRENT ACCOUNT IMBALANCES, THE WORLD CAPITAL MARKET AND THE REAL INTEREST RATE

It is likely that most of the countries present current account imbalances, that is $X - M \neq 0$. As is easy to show from the aggregate demand expression, this imbalance corresponds to a divergence between internal savings (both private and public) and investments (again both private and public): a current account deficit implies that the country is actually borrowing from the rest of the world since its national savings are insufficient to finance its investments whereas a current account surplus reveals that the country is lending to the rest of the world. These divergences, present at the national level, cancel out at the world level: funds' demands and supplies are conveyed and traded in an international capital market where the world real rate of interest is determined.

The real interest rate is a key factor in any inter-temporal choice. Hence we expect it to play a meaningful role in the firm's price, production and investment decisions, in the households' consumption/saving decisions and in the public sector's policies.

The endogenization of the real interest rate, however, impinges on controversial theoretical grounds. The origins of the debate go back to Fisher, who conceived the concept of 'real rate of interest', and to Friedman and Keynes who held quite different opinions concerning the degree of liquidity of money and hence its substitutability with real assets.

Today the post-Keynesian school still denies the relevance of the real interest rate; on the other hand they claim that it is the nominal interest rate, actually observed in the economy,[13] the rate which agents look at in order to make their decisions. Other scholars, though not refusing the importance of the real rate of interest, maintain that its determinants are merely those of the nominal rate of interest and of expected inflation; according to others the real interest rate is constant and changes in the nominal interest rate reflect changes in expected inflation (Fisher, 1930).[14]

Studies on the real rate of interest have grown particularly numerous during the 1980s when the real interest rate soared to unusually high levels and remained high for a long period. Most of these studies are essentially empirical investigations on the determinants of the real interest rate and are based on a theoretical framework analogous to the one proposed here according to which the real rate of interest is determined in the capital market by equating world savings to world investments (see for example Barro and Sala-i-Martin 1990; Blanchard and Summers 1986; Bruno and Sachs 1985; Mishkin 1993).

It is clear however that such a theoretical basis, which well fits a strictly neoclassical approach where prices and wages are perfectly flexible and perfect competition prevails, must be properly extended if a more general background is considered. In the neoclassical case, where production is fixed at the full employment level, changes in the capital market and in the real interest rate exclusively determine changes in the composition of aggregate demand. However, in a more Keynesian approach, where production may fall below full employment and aggregate demand may affect the level of income, the saving–investment market must be considered in conjunction with the supply side.

As we saw in the first chapter, the unfolding of the real rate of interest in the decades under consideration is marked by sharp changes: after remaining fairly constant until the end of the 1960s, it declined to negative values in the early 1970s and then rose to nearly two digit numbers in the early 1980s (see Figure 2.3).

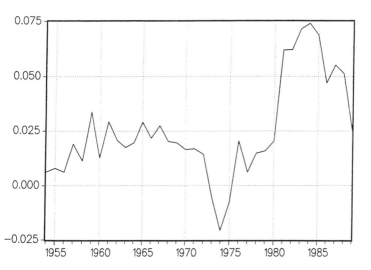

Figure 2.3 OECD real rate of interest

Among the causes leading to the high real interest rate much attention has been paid to US monetary and fiscal policy; outside the OECD, instead, the LDC external debt, which soared in the early 1980s as a consequence of restrictive policies successively became a dangerous boomerang for the capital market. We will return to this topic in Chapter 4.

Since the current account deficit/surplus reflects the domestic shortage/excess of savings, only one of these two sides of the same imbalance is to be considered in the determination of the real interest rate.

The equation of the real rate of interest is derived by equating the world total savings (that is, OECD private and public savings plus current account surpluses of LDC economies, mainly oil exporting countries) with the world total investment or financial funds' demand (that is, private and public OECD investments plus the current accounts of those LDC economies showing a deficit position, mainly oil importing countries). The response of the capital market to demand and supply of funds, however, is conditional on past imbalances, typically represented by the LDC external debt and by OECD government debts. The real interest rate equation, as derived in Chapter 3, then looks as follows:

$$
\begin{aligned}
R = c_8 + a_8 y - d_8 U - e_8 \Delta p &- g_8(pc - p) - h_8 y^* - i_8 T \\
&+ l_8(g - p) - m_8(m - p) + n_8 \Pi^e + p_8(s - p) \\
&+ q_8(e - p)
\end{aligned}
\tag{2.11}
$$

where s is the log of LDC external debt and e is the log of OECD government debt.

Whereas the OECD monetary and fiscal policies can quite safely be assumed to be exogenous policy instruments, the external imbalances of many LDC countries clearly need a further endogenization. The debt crisis had much to do with the tight policies enforced by the industrialized countries, the high real interest rate and the second oil price rise; therefore, in order to grasp the complete working of the financial market the latter must be extended to include a function explaining the evolution of the LDC current account deficit.

2.7 THE EVOLUTION OF THE LDC EXTERNAL DEBT

As we commented in the previous chapter, the early 1980s LDC debt crisis has its origin in the preceding decade. In the 1970s many LDC countries were borrowing from abroad in order to finance important public investment projects.[15] Following the first oil shock many oil-importing LDC countries decided to extend their borrowing in order to pay the higher oil bills.[16]

Two important facts made it possible for the LDC to obtain such an extensive borrowing: the set-up, in 1957, of the Eurodollar market in London, which provided short-term lending in dollars and to which, by the early 1970s, most developing countries had access and some elongation of the debt maturity offered by many banks.

Moreover the sharp increase of the price of oil determined a huge transfer of income from industrialized oil-importing to oil-exporting countries; as the latter were unable to spend all the revenues, excess savings generated fresh liquidity available in large amounts and provoked a decline of the rate of interest. In this period bank lending grew further and the level of external borrowing of many countries soared. However it was not until the second oil shock that the danger of such a financial exposure was fully realized.

The circumstances in which the second oil shock took place were quite different from those of the early 1970s: the level of external borrowing was much higher and the restrictive policies adopted by OECD oil-importing countries were much more severe; 1979 also marked a change in the US Federal Reserve policy whose target shifted from the interest rate to money supply determining higher nominal interest rates. This background, coupled with the fact that most of the bank debt was short term determined growing difficulties for the borrowing countries which culminated with the Mexico default in 1982.

Highly indebted developing countries, faced with this crisis, were forced to raise their revenues in order to service burgeoning interest. It has been argued that these countries tried to reduce the price of their exports, that is, the price of primary commodities. Evidence of this is found by Aizenman and Borensztien (1988), Gilbert (1989a), Borensztein and Reinhart (1994). We will return to this topic when discussing the primary commodity price equation.

As shown in detail in the next chapter, the evolution over time of the LDC external debt is determined by the non-interest current account deficit plus the interest to be served on past debt, less financial aid from the North. The latter are assumed to be positively dependent on Northern output but to be negatively affected by the real interest rate and the level of existing debt. Using the current account definitions introduced for aggregate demand, the evolution of LDC real external debt over time then looks as follows:

$$\Delta(s - p) = c_9 - a_9 y + b_9 R + g_9(pc - p) + h_9 y^* + i_9(s - p)_{-1}$$

$$(2.12)$$

The empirical estimation of this equation may encounter some difficulties as long as the debt crisis of the early 1980s produced a structural break; if two regimes are indeed present, then a single equation would yield unstable coefficients. In the empirical version the impact of each explanatory variable is therefore allowed to change between the pre- and the post-default period.

2.8   THE PRIMARY COMMODITY MARKET

Within the primary commodity market, endogenization is pursued for the non-oil primary commodity price component alone.[17] The latter we consider as an aggregate index, hence the standard theory of commodity price formation, which is developed for a single commodity, is not expected to apply exactly; rather it is used as a general guide to a coherent empirical specification.

Primary commodity prices are typically highly homogeneous and for many of them transport and storage costs are relatively low. These features imply two important characteristics of primary commodities:

1. they are normally traded in competitive markets (Labys, 1980); and
2. they are traded in international markets and to some respect are similar to financial assets.

The determination of the price of a single commodity is normally based on a standard structural model in which demand and supply are specified. When considering an aggregate index of commodities a reduced form is usually employed. The latter is determined (see Gilbert, 1988, 1989*b*) from the market clearing condition according to which:

$$Q_c + F_{-1} = C_c + F \qquad (2.13)$$

that is, production of commodity (Q_c) plus past storage (F_{-1}) equals demand (C_c) plus present stockholding demand (F).

Given the presence of stockholding, an optimal inventory condition needs to be introduced. The latter is usually specified in two alternative ways (Deaton and Laroque, 1990). The easiest function to implement empirically and hence the one most widely used in empirical studies defines a linear inventory demand; the alternative, on the contrary, specifies a non-linear function since it assumes a non-negativity constraint for inventories. If risk neutrality is approached or, equivalently, if the risk is completely diversified, the two cases coincide as long as stockholding is positive.

The importance of the non-negativity constraint is clear for agricultural products and for non-agricultural commodities as long as storage costs are not negligible. As discussed in detail in the next chapter, the non-negativity constraint allows the price of primary commodities to behave asymmetrically with sharp high rises and long downs, a path that well resembles that of a typical commodity price.

At least for this reason, apart from its empirical tractability, the use of a linear function is arguable; however its usage for aggregated commodity indices is less controversial since it can be assumed that in aggregate some stocks are always held. Indeed for many commodities (for example mineral and metals) warehousing costs and deterioration are negligible and production is a continuous process rather than a discrete one; harvest seasons differ across products and convenience yield may be important.

The aggregate primary commodity price equation is therefore obtained by specifying demand and supply of primary commodities as functions of both price and non-price factors and then using such equations together with a linear stock demand function.

Following the wealth of literature existing on the topic, the basic specification is extended in several important ways, as explained in detail in Chapter 3. The final commodity price equation is specified according to an ECM; leaving aside dynamics, the steady-state commodity price equation can therefore be viewed as a function of the following variables:

$$pn_t - p_t = c_{10} + b_{10} R_t - d_{10} U - e_{10}(s - p) + f_{10}(po - p)$$

$$(2.14)$$

As anticipated in Section 2.7, the presence of the LDC external debt among the explanatory variables of the non-oil primary commodity price equation rests on the reaction of highly indebted developing countries to the 1980s crisis.

However, though a negative effect of debt on the price of primaries has been advocated by several authors,[18] the roots of this relationship do not appear unilaterally determined. According to one view this effect is linked to the well-known negative response of primary commodity prices to a rise in the value of the dollar. Since the absolute value of this response is empirically greater than that theoretically expected, commodity exporting countries, whose imports are primarily US manufactured goods, are thereby impoverished. As pointed out by Van Wijnbergen (1985) this disadvantage worsens in the presence of a growing dollar-dominated external debt. Gilbert (1989a) formalizes this argument and suggests that the observed excess sensitivity of commodity prices to changes in the dollar may be induced by large external debts in primary commodity producing LDCs.[19]

Others argue, instead, that, faced with the debt crisis, developing countries started increasing their supply of primary commodities and such a surge depressed the price (Aizenman and Borensztien, 1988, Borensztein and Reinhart, 1994). Given our specification of the commodity price equation the two views are observationally equivalent and we cannot distinguish between them.

None the less the link they emphasize remains very important and introduces a two-way relationship between LDC external debt and primary commodity prices.

2.9   THE WORKING OF THE MODEL

We can now proceed to the overall view of the model represented by equations (2.1), (2.2), (2.3), (2.4), (2.6), (2.9), (2.10), (2.11), (2.12) and (2.14). To these behavioural relationships two identities are attached: the first one is equation (2.5), which links the rate of unemployment to the log of employment and labour force, the second one defines the aggregate primary commodity price index as a weighted average of oil and non-oil commodity price indices:[20]

$$pc = \alpha pn + (1 - \alpha)po \tag{2.15}$$

where α is the share of non-oil commodity imports from developing countries and po is the price of oil.

The model is therefore composed of 10 behavioural equations plus two identities and solves for twelve variables in the whole: p, w, NC/N, l, n, y, y^*, R, s, pn, pc and U. This standard solution, which we call the short-run or dynamic solution, is also used to perform simulations.

In addition, we compute the long-run or equilibrium solution, which, as usual, identifies that particular point in time in which expectations are realized and there is no incentive to adjust. In this case variables are all determined in *real* terms; the long-run solution determines the real wage $(w - p)$, which equals the opposite of the price mark-up over wages $(p - w)$, $NC/N, n, l, y, y^*, R, (s - p), (pn - p), (pc - p), U$ and $(m - p)$; the possibility to determine a further variable, which we chose to be the real money supply but which could equally be another one of the short-run exogenous variables, is due to the equality between the real wage and the opposite of the price mark-up over wages (that is: $w - p = -(p - w)$).

The distinction between the short- and the long-run is an important one since it permits discussion of the divergences between the actual and the equilibrium paths of the endogenous variables; we will employ this distinction throughout the empirical work.

In practice the long-run system looks much simpler than its dynamic counterpart since all adjustment processes are completed. Therefore, in order to describe the functioning of the overall model it is preferable to start from the long-run solution.

For ease of exposition, the following re-arrangements are made: in the wage equation the normalized industrial conflicts are replaced by their function and in the primary commodity price equation and in the real interest rate equation, LDC external debt is replaced by its expression; this allows us to concentrate on four basic equations: price, wage, primary commodity and real interest rate. In these equations short-run demand factors, whose relevance is normally linked to the operation of partial adjustment mechanisms, are made explicit. Notice here that, since there exists a linear inverse relationship between deviations of production from trend and U,[21] we can take U as the OECD demand indicator and hence include ΔU as the short-run demand variable.

The price, the wage, the primary commodity and the real interest rate equations then look as follows:

$$p - w = \bar{c}_2 + \bar{b}_2 R - \bar{d}_2 U - \bar{d}_{21} \Delta U + \bar{e}_2(p - p^e) - \bar{f}_2(w - w^e)$$

$$(2.16)$$

$$w - p = \bar{c}_3 - \bar{b}_3 R - \bar{d}_3 U - \bar{d}_{31} \Delta U - \bar{e}_3(p - p^e) + \bar{f}_3(w - w^e)$$
$$+ \bar{g}_3(pc - p) \tag{2.17}$$

$$R = \bar{c}_8 - \bar{d}_8 U - \bar{d}_{81} \Delta U + \bar{g}_8(pc - p) \tag{2.18}$$

$$pn_t - p_t = \bar{c}_{10} + \bar{b}_{10} R_t - \bar{d}_{10} U - \bar{d}_{101} \Delta U + \bar{f}_{10}(po - p) \tag{2.19}$$

$$U = l - n \tag{2.20}$$

$$pc = \alpha pn + (1 - \alpha)po \tag{2.21}$$

where, for convenience, exogenous variables and trend productivity are grouped in the constant term and a bar on the coefficients indicates that they may differ from the original ones since the expressions are now partial reduced forms.

This simplified model is used to illustrate the essential interactions between the endogenous variables of interest and understand the role of short-run factors in originating the divergence of actual paths from the equilibrium.

2.9.1 The long-run solution

The functioning of the OECD supply side has been delineated in Section 2.4. In order to picture the equilibrium of the complete model, that is an equilibrium comprehensive of the links between the OECD and the primary commodity market, an extended approach needs to be devised.

In order to do this, two relationships linking U and $(pn - p)$ are identified. One of this ultimately embodies the equilibrium in the North, the other one the equilibrium in the South. To obtain the first relation the wage and the price equations (2.17) and (2.16) are equated with price and wage surprises set to zero and then solved for $(pn - p)$ using identity (2.15). The second relationship stems directly from the primary commodity price equation (2.19).

Let us first consider the long run where, by definition, all adjustments are completed. The equation representing the relationship between primary commodity price and the rate of unemployment stemming from the North is the following:

$$pn - p = -\frac{C}{G\alpha} + \frac{B}{G\alpha}R + \frac{D}{G\alpha}U - \frac{(1-\alpha)}{\alpha}(po - p) \qquad (2.22)$$

where $C = \bar{c}_3 + \bar{c}_2, B = \bar{b}_3 - \bar{b}_2, G = \bar{g}_3, D = \bar{d}_3 + \bar{d}_2$
and the long-run reduced form primary commodity price equation is:

$$pn_t - p_t = \bar{c}_{10} + \bar{b}_{10}R_t - \bar{d}_{10}U + \bar{f}_{10}(po - p) \qquad (2.23)$$

Equations (2.22) and (2.23) permit us to draw, in the $U - (pn - p)$ space, two lines whose intersection determines the equilibrium rate of unemployment and the equilibrium non-oil real primary commodity price. If these equations were already solved for R and for the remaining endogenous variables, then the equilibrium point they identify, being conditional on exogenous variables only, would be the 'general' equilibrium of the model. In this case we would refer to these lines as unconditional 'North' and 'South' lines: they are pictured in figure 2.4. Notice that we may think of the 'North' and 'South' lines as 'demand' and 'supply' functions where the rate of unemployment is assumed to be inversely related to the quantity demanded and supplied.

Recall that the North line is the locus of points of equilibrium for the North, that is points in which the price and the wage equation intersect and no surprises are present. Hence, by following the discussion on the functioning of the OECD supply side we can say that points to the left of U^* in the wage–price diagram, where inflation is rising, correspond to points above the North line; otherwise points to the right of U^* in the wage–price diagram, correspond to points below the North line where inflation is declining.

In other words points above the North line entail, for a given $(pn - p)$, a lower than equilibrium rate of unemployment (hence excess demand and rising inflation); likewise points below the North line entail, for a given $(pn - p)$, a higher than equilibrium rate of unemployment (hence excess supply and falling inflation).

The lines depicted in Figure 2.4 are not yet rooted on the evidence: the actual empirical counterpart of these lines will be

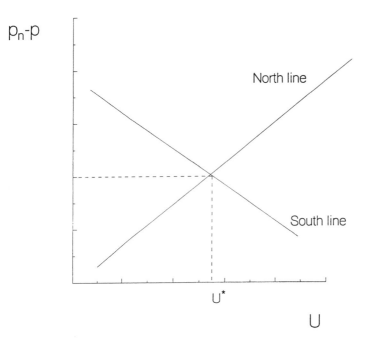

Figure 2.4 North-South equilibrium

drawn in chapter 4 on the basis of the estimated model. Indeed the slopes of the North and South lines could be very different from those sketched, depending on the relevance of the various markets, on their functioning and on their interaction. At this regard it is interesting to compare the unconditional North and South lines with those which still condition on some endogenous variable and hence represent a partial equilibrium situation. For example, it is easy to verify that, by replacing R by its function, the North line, for particular values of the coefficients,[22] could be negatively sloped; in this case stability would be preserved as long as the North line remains steeper than the South line; likewise the South line could be positively sloped, in which case, for the system to be stable, the South line must be steeper than the North line.

Now, consider, for example, a positive shock on commodity prices, for example a once-and-for-all oil price increase. In the $U - (w - p)$ space, the wage line shifts rightwards and correspondingly, in the $U - (pn - p)$ space, the North and South lines move rightwards. The effect on the overall equilibrium rate of unemployment depends on the relative slopes of the two lines. If the North line is upward sloping and the South line is downward sloping, as we expect for reasonable values of the parameters, the rate of unemployment increases; the same is true if both lines are upward sloping and stability is preserved; however, if both lines are downward sloping, the unemployment rate could even decline.[23]

This is significant since it shows how the endogenization of important macroeconomic variables may change the final response of the dependent variables[24] and proves that the framework used is capable of capturing the a priori ambiguity rounding the final impact of exogenous commodity price shock on the North's economic activity as we discussed in chapter 1. The empirical implementation of the model will verify this possibility.

2.9.2   A comparison between the long- and the short-run

Since the North line is defined as the locus of point consistent with no surprises in the North, the short-run analysis extends the previous one for the presence of those short-run factors ascribable to partial adjustment mechanisms linked, in turn, to adjustment costs, incompleteness of the information set, imperfections of the markets.

When short-run factors are considered the North and the South lines become respectively:

$$pn - p = -\frac{C}{\alpha G} + \frac{B}{\alpha G}R + \frac{(D + D_1)}{\alpha G}U - \frac{(1 - \alpha)}{\alpha}(po - p)$$
$$-\frac{D_1}{\alpha G}U_{-1} \tag{2.24}$$

where, $D_1 = \bar{d}_{31} + \bar{d}_{32}$

and

$$pn_t - p_t = \bar{c}_{10} + \bar{b}_{10} R_t - (\bar{d}_{10} + \bar{d}_{101})U + \bar{d}_{101}U_{-1} + \bar{f}_{10}(po - p) \tag{2.25}$$

Notice first of all that the long- and the short-run lines intersect at $U = U_{-1}$.

Moreover, it is easy to verify that, as long as the coefficients of ΔU have the same sign as the coefficients of U, the short-run lines are steeper than their long-run counterparts. In this case, the responses of prices to shocks are sharper in the short-run than in the long-run but the responses of quantities are smaller in the short-run. This implies that a policy aimed at reducing the rate of unemployment is more costly, in terms of inflation, in the short-run than it is in the long-run; on the contrary, the sacrifice in terms of unemployment required to cut down inflation is smaller in the short-run than it is in the long-run. Likewise, exogenous changes in the primary commodity market which shift the short-run South line upwards have a relatively weaker impact on U whereas OECD exogenous shocks which shift the short-run North line downwards have a reinforced effect on primary prices.

Figure 2.5 depicts a comparison between the short- and the long-run in the case just described: notice that at the point of intersection between the short-run wage and price lines, forecasting errors are absent; hence this point identifies the current rate of unemployment associated with no change in inflation: we shall call it 'short-run equilibrium rate of unemployment', U^{*S}.

At rates of unemployment lower than U^{*S}, the gap between wage and price is positive; in order to reduce it and lead the system back to equilibrium, forecasting errors must decrease, that is inflation must decline relative to the expectations. On the contrary, levels of U above U^{*S} correspond to a negative gap, hence the necessity to raise prediction errors to bring back the equilibrium, that is inflation must increase relative to the expectations: this is basically the Phillips curve mechanism.

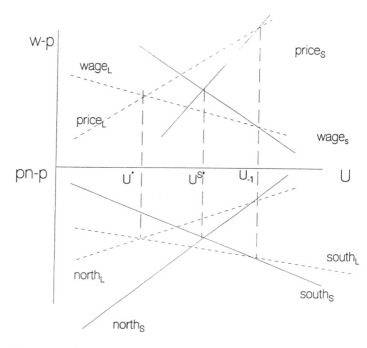

Figure 2.5   Short- and long-run lines

Notice also that in Figure 2.5 the short-run equilibrium rate of unemployment is higher than its long-run analogue; this case arises if the intercepts of the short-run lines, which are greater than the intercepts of the long-run lines,[25] assume very large values (because of large values of U_{-1} and/or of the coefficients $\bar{d}_{21}$ and $\bar{d}_{31}$); in practice, given the coefficients, $U^{S*} \geq U^*$ depending on $U_{-1} \geq U^*$. The case depicted is the most interesting one since it well illustrates the problems which may arise if the economy operates above its long-run equilibrium rate of unemployment but below its short-run equilibrium one; in particular, as it is clear from Figure 2.5, it exemplifies how the current rate of unemployment relates to its past value and to its equilibrium.

2.9.3 The sources of hysteresis: nominal inertia

An important aspect of the short-run model relates to the sources of its potential persistence, a feature that has attracted vast attention particularly since it was linked to the recent developments of the OECD unemployment rate (Blanchard and Summers, 1986).

In order to analyse nominal inertia it is useful to make the following assumptions, based on empirical facts:

1. wage forecasting errors are a linear function of price forecasting errors, that is:

$$(w - w^e) = \gamma(p - p^e), \gamma > 0$$

2. price forecasting errors are a linear function of changes in inflation, that is:

$$(p - p^e) = \varphi \Delta^2 p, \varphi > 0$$

Then, by equating price and wage equation and solving for $(p - p^e)$ we obtain:

$$(p - p^e) = \frac{1}{(\bar{e}_3 - \bar{e}_2 + \gamma(\bar{f}_2 - \bar{f}_3))}((\bar{c}_3 + \bar{c}_2) - (\bar{b}_3 - \bar{b}_2)R$$
$$+ \bar{g}_3(pc - p) - (\bar{d}_3 + \bar{d}_2)U - (\bar{d}_{31} + \bar{d}_{21})\Delta U)$$
$$(2.26)$$

By using the symbols already introduced and letting $\bar{e}_3 - \bar{e}_2 + \gamma(\bar{f}_2 - \bar{f}_3) = E$, equation (2.26) may also be written as follows:

$$(p - p^e) = \frac{C}{E} - \frac{B}{E}R + \frac{G}{E}(pc - p) - \frac{D}{E}U - \frac{D_1}{E}\Delta U \qquad (2.27)$$

This equation can be simplified by noting that equilibrium in the North entails: $-C + BR - G(pc - p) = -DU^*$ where U^* is the long-run equilibrium rate of unemployment conditional on $(pc - p)$ and R. Then equation (2.27) becomes:

$$\varphi \Delta^2 p = (p - p^e) = -\frac{D}{E}(U - U^*) - \frac{D_1}{E}\Delta U \qquad (2.28)$$

This equation illustrates that, even in absence of short-run pressure from primary prices, short-run demand factors alone could drive inflation by dominating the forces of the long-run factors. In order to see this, let us equate $\Delta^2 p$ to zero and draw the constant change of inflation line in the $\Delta U - U$ space:

$$U = U^* - \frac{D_1}{D} \Delta U \tag{2.29}$$

Figure 2.6 illustrates; above the line inflation is falling ($\Delta^2 p < 0$) and below it is rising ($\Delta^2 p > 0$).

The shaded areas represent situations in which the *change* of the rate of unemployment dominates the *level* in determining the rate of change of inflation: a falling (rising) rate of unemployment increases (decreases) inflation even if the rate of unemployment is above (below) its equilibrium; such cases are more probable the larger the coefficient of the short-run factors D_1 relative to D.

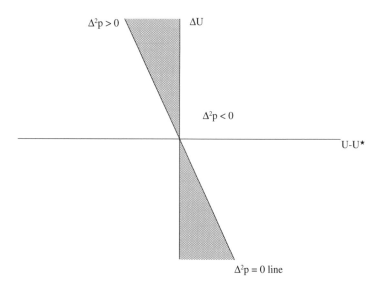

Figure 2.6   Constant change of inflation line

The empirical version of equation (2.28) is presented in Chapter 4.

2.9.4 The sources of hysteresis: short-run factors

To investigate the sources of hysteresis we start from the procedure described in Layard *et al.* (1991) and extend it in order to verify what happens when primary commodity prices and the world real interest rate are endogenized.

The case of exogenous primary commodity prices and real interest rate is the basic one from which to start; then the current rate of unemployment associated with no changes in inflation, that is the short-run equilibrium rate of unemployment U^{S*} as we called it, is given by solving equation (2.29) in terms of U:

$$U^{*S} = \frac{D}{(D + D_1)} U^* + \frac{D_1}{(D + D_1)} U_{-1} \tag{2.30}$$

Equation (2.30) tells us that the higher the short-run factor coefficient D_1 relative to that of long-run factors, D, the closer the short-run equilibrium rate of unemployment to its level in the past period (U_{-1}). We may add that in this case, as suggested by Figure 2.6, it is likely to observe rising inflation associated with $U > U^*$ but negative ΔU.

By endogenizing non-oil primary prices the expression for the short-run equilibrium rate of unemployment becomes:

$$U^{*S} = \frac{\alpha G \bar{d}_{10} + D}{\alpha G(\bar{d}_{10} + \bar{d}_{101}) + (D + D_1)} U^{**}$$
$$+ \frac{\alpha G \bar{d}_{101} + D_1}{\alpha G(\bar{d}_{10} + \bar{d}_{101}) + (D + D_1)} U_{-1} \tag{2.31}$$

where the long-run equilibrium rate of unemployment, U^{**}, is now conditional on the real rate of interest only:

$$U^{**} = \frac{C + \alpha G \bar{c}_{10} + (\alpha G \bar{b}_{10} - B) R + G(\alpha \bar{f}_{10} + 1 - \alpha)(po - p)}{\alpha G \bar{d}_{10} + D}$$

Equation (2.31) shows that by accounting for external factors (like primary prices) the conclusion of the initial partial equilibrium case may be reverted; in particular short-run internal demand factors (D_1) are no longer necessary nor sufficient for hysteresis to appear. Suppose, for example, that $D_1 = 0$ and $D = 1$ but $d_{101} = 1$ and $d_{10} = 0$; then, if $G \neq 0$, hysteresis is present whereas in the partial equilibrium case this would produce no hysteresis at all, that is $U^{*S} = U^*$.

Finally, let us endogenize the real interest rate; the short-run equilibrium rate of unemployment then reads as follows:

$$U^{*S} = \frac{\alpha(G - B\bar{g}_8)(\bar{b}_{10}\bar{d}_{81} + \bar{d}_{101}) + (1 - \bar{b}_{10}\bar{g}_8\alpha)(D_1 - B\bar{d}_{81})}{Z}U_{-1}$$
$$+ \frac{\alpha(G - B\bar{g}_8)(\bar{b}_{10}\bar{d}_8 + \bar{d}_{10}) + (1 - \bar{b}_{10}\bar{g}_8\alpha)(D - B\bar{d}_8)}{Z}U^{***}$$

where $Z = \alpha(G - B\bar{g}_8)(\bar{b}_{10}(\bar{d}_8 + \bar{d}_{81}) + (\bar{d}_{10} + \bar{d}_{101}))$
$+ (D + D_1) - B(\bar{d}_8 + \bar{d}_{81})(1 - \bar{b}_{10}\bar{g}_8\alpha)$

where U^{***} is the long-run equilibrium rate of unemployment conditional on oil prices only.

Notice that in this case if both $D_1 = 0$ and $\bar{d}_{101} = 1$, that is if hysteresis elements are absent in the North supply-side as well as in the primary commodity market, still hysteresis may arise if short-run factors are present in the financial market. However the working of the latter may either fuel or hinder hysteresis, depending on the sign of the real interest rate in the unemployment equation (i.e. the sign of B). Finally observe that an additional channel through which hysteresis may spread via the financial market is through the impact of the latter on the primary commodities (the coefficient g_8 in the above equation).

In chapter 4, using the estimated model, we will be able to estimate equations (2.30), (2.31) and (2.32) and investigate to what extent the persistence of the rate of unemployment is affected by internal factors, primary commodity prices and the real interest rate.

3 Details of the Model

The OECD economy is modelled in detail: the demand and the supply side are made explicit in an imperfectly competitive framework. The description of the LDC region is based on an aggregate demand function; however the evolution of the LDC foreign debt over time, which contributes to the performance of the international financial market and the endogenization of the primary commodity market, enhance the representativeness of the Southern block.

3.1 THE OECD PRODUCTION FUNCTION AND PRICE EQUATION

The OECD economy is exemplified by N identical imperfectly competitive firms which face a downward sloping demand curve and jointly decide the quantity to produce and the selling price. Output is planned on the basis of expected aggregate demand in proportion to a factor which depends on the firm's relative price and market share. Since production starts before demand is realized, planned production is equal to the actual one using inventories, if necessary, to meet actual demand. Hence we have:

$$\bar{Q}_i = Y^e \Omega_i \tag{3.1}$$

and

$$\Omega_i = \left(\frac{P_i}{P^e}\right)^{-\varepsilon} \left(\frac{SAL_i}{SAL}\right)^{\delta} \tag{3.2}$$

where $\bar{Q}$ is planned output, Y^e is expected aggregate demand, P is output price and P^e is the expected output price, ε and δ are the price elasticities to demand and to market share

respectively, SAL are sales and subscript i denotes the firms
By summing over firms we obtain:

$$\bar{Q} = Y^e(P/P^e)^{-\varepsilon} = Q = Y(P/P^e)^{-\varepsilon}(\Delta D/D)^{\sigma} \qquad (3.3)$$

where Q is actual output, D are inventories and σ is a positive
parameter linking deviations of demand from expectations to
changes in inventories.[1]

Following the profit maximizing rationale, the price of output is
set in order to cover the expected marginal variable costs plus a
mark-up which we take to be potentially subject to cyclical
movements. The response of the mark up over the business
cycle and its magnitude are questions that go back to Keynes
(1939) and Kalecki (1938) and still remain, both theoretically
and empirically, unresolved. Because of the important issues
involved (the explanation of the cyclical movements in real
wages, for example), the behaviour of the product market
continues to command attention among macroeconomists. In a
meticulous paper Rotemberg and Woodford (1991) review three
main theoretical approaches to the determination of the mark-
up: the static monopolistic competition model, the customer
market model (Phelps and Winter, 1970; Phelps, 1994) and the
implicit collusion model (Rotemberg and Soloner, 1986;
Rotemberg and Woodford, 1992).

Given the degree of aggregation employed, our model cannot
produce evidence in favour of either theory but it needs to
be sufficiently comprehensive to capture the different price
determination mechanisms working within the OECD economy.

Starting from the standard monopoly case it is easy to show
that the mark-up over marginal costs is a negative function of
the elasticity of demand facing the firm;[2] following the
arguments put forward by Rotenberg and Woodford (1991)
we take the latter to respond to deviations of demand from its
trend. When the elasticity of demand tends to infinity the
perfect competitive case is recovered.

Both oligopolistic considerations, stemming from the collusion model, and investment-like considerations, which are
distinctive of the customer market model, imply the inclusion

of dynamics. The discounted flow of future profits is an important determinant of today's price decisions: it is the foregone gain for the deviators in the collusion model and the future benefit with which present profits are traded-off in the customer model. However, changes in the present discounted value of profits have opposite effects on the mark-up in the two theories: a rise of future profits lowers the mark-up in the costumer model but rises it in the implicit collusion one in order to preserve equilibrium. In our model we take the real interest rate to represent the importance attached to the future, so that we expect a positive sign according to Phelps and Winter's model and a negative one according to Rotenberg–Soloner–Woodford's approach.

Using the rate of unemployment to approximate deviations of demand from trend,[3] the price function can then be written as follows:

$$P_i = \mu(R, U)MC_i^e \tag{3.4}$$

where μ is the mark-up, R is the real interest rate, U is the rate of unemployment and MC^e is the expected marginal cost.[4]

In order to obtain an expression for the marginal cost we introduce the available technique represented by the following value-added production function:

$$\bar{Q}_i = f_1(\bar{N}_i, K_i, A_i) \tag{3.5}$$

where $\bar{N}$ is planned employment, A is an index of technical progress and capital is given; the amount of employment required to produce the planned quantity of output is simply obtained by inverting (3.5).

However, the labour force actually employed may differ from $\bar{N}$ because of binding constraints due to labour market mismatch (in which case $N < \bar{N}$) or because the firm is hoarding labour (in which case $N > \bar{N}$); we assume that these short-run discrepancies are adjusted by deviations of working hours from trend $(H/\bar{H})$ so that:

$$\bar{N}_i = g_1(N_i, (H/\bar{H})_i) \tag{3.6}$$

Hence:

$$\bar{Q}_i = f_2(N_i, (H/\bar{H})_i, K_i, A_i) \tag{3.7}$$

The empirical version of the model assumes a log-linear production function; by aggregating over firms and taking logarithms, denoted by small letters, equation (3.7) becomes:

$$\bar{q}_t = a_t + \alpha n_t + \beta k_t + \xi(h - \bar{h})_t \tag{3.8}$$

where α, β, ξ are the factors' shares in production.

Since the expected marginal cost is the product of the expected wage W^e and the desired inverse marginal product of labour $\frac{\partial \bar{N}}{\partial \bar{Q}}$, we use the production function to compute the latter:

$$\begin{aligned}
\ln(\partial \bar{N}/\partial \bar{Q}) &= \ln(1/\alpha) + \ln \bar{N} - \ln \bar{Q} \\
&= \ln(1/\alpha) + \ln \bar{N} - \ln Y^e + \varepsilon \ln(P/P^e) \qquad (3.9) \\
&= \ln(1/\alpha) + \ln N + \xi \ln(H/\bar{H}) - \ln Y^e + \varepsilon \ln(P/P^e)
\end{aligned}$$

where planned output and planned employment have been substituted out using, respectively, (3.3) and (3.6).[5] Expression (3.9) can be usefully re-formulated using the labour force L:

$$\begin{aligned}
\ln(\partial \bar{N}/\partial \bar{Q}) = {} & \ln(1/\alpha) - \ln(L/N) + \xi \ln(H/\bar{H}) - \ln(Y^e/L) \\
& + \varepsilon \ln(P/P^e) \qquad (3.9')
\end{aligned}$$

This is an interesting re-arrangement since it splits the inverse of the marginal product of labour into cyclical components, captured by the rate of unemployment and by deviations of working hours from trend, a trending component, captured by a measure of trend productivity and a final component linked to unexpected price changes.[6]

Finally, the price equation is derived by substituting the expected marginal cost into equation (3.4):

$$\begin{aligned}
p - w = {} & \rho_0 R - \rho_1 U - (w - w^e) + \ln(1/\alpha) - U \\
& + \xi(h - \bar{h}) - (y^e - l) + \varepsilon(p - p^e) \qquad (3.10)
\end{aligned}$$

where ρ_0 and ρ_1 are the coefficients capturing the impact of R and U on the mark-up and, as usual, small letters denote logarithms.

The lag structure of this equation, which presumes the presence of adjustments costs, is determined empirically.

3.2 THE OECD LABOUR MARKET

In order to obtain a sufficiently general representation of the OECD labour market, three institutionally different labour markets are considered: one dominated by demand and supply, another one driven by efficiency wage considerations and the last one characterized by the presence of insiders or groups of insiders possibly organized in unions.

3.2.1 The competitive model

In the market-dominated model labour supply N^s is a positive function of the take home consumption wage, given the labour force L:

$$N^s = L(\bar{W}/P_{co})^\eta = L\left(\frac{W(1 - T_1 - T_2)}{Pc^\chi P^{(1-\chi)}}\right)^\eta \tag{3.11}$$

where $\bar{W}$ is the after tax wage, P_{co} are consumer prices, η the real wage elasticity of labour supply, χ the import share in gross output, T_1 and T_2 the tax rates borne by the households and the firm respectively, Pc are import prices in OECD currency[7] and the remaining symbols are as previously defined. Transforming into logarithms and re-arranging we get:

$$\ln N^s = \ln L + \eta \ln(W/P) - \eta(T_1 + T_2) - \eta\chi \ln(Pc/P) \tag{3.12}$$

Labour demand is obtained from the profit maximizing condition (3.10) by recalling that $U = \ln L - \ln N$:

$$\ln N^d = \frac{1}{(1 + \rho_1)}\Big(-\ln(W/P) - \ln 1/A + \ln Y^e - \xi \ln(H/\bar{H})$$
$$- \rho_0 \cdot R + \rho_1 \ln L - \varepsilon \ln(P/P^e) + \ln(W/W^e)\Big) \tag{3.13}$$

The logarithm of the competitive real wage $(w - p)^c$ is finally obtained by equating demand and supply:

$$(w-p)^C = \left(\eta + \frac{1}{(1+\rho_1)}\right)^{-1} \left\{ -\frac{1}{(1+\rho_1)}\ln(1/\alpha) + \frac{1}{(1+\rho_1)}(y^e - l) \right.$$
$$- \frac{\xi}{(1+\rho_1)}(h - \bar{h}) - \frac{\rho_0}{(1+\rho_1)}R - \frac{\varepsilon}{(1+\rho_1)}(p - p^e)$$
$$\left. + \frac{1}{(1+\rho_1)}(w - w^e) + \eta(T_1 + T_2) + \eta\chi(pc - p) \right\}$$

$$(3.14)$$

3.2.2   The efficiency wage model

The situation where the firm can unilaterally set the wage is represented by the efficiency wage model according to which the wage is set in order to induce a given effort or productivity on the part of the workers. A standard efficiency wage model (Solow, 1979) defines labour input in terms of effort and derives the wage from the profit maximization condition. For any effort function $e(\cdot)$, dependent on the real wage, and production function $F(\cdot)$, real profits Π/P are given by:

$$\frac{\Pi}{P} = AF(eNH, K) - \frac{WN}{P}$$

$$(3.15)$$

The first order condition for profit maximization with respect to the real wage yields:

$$A\frac{\partial F}{\partial e}\frac{\partial e}{\partial(W/P)} = 1$$

$$(3.16)$$

In order to derive the wage equation the effort function must be specified; to keep things simple we assume that aggregate effort is positively related to the actual real wage relative to expected earnings outside the firm:

$$e = \left(\frac{W/P}{(W^e/P)^{(1-U)}(B/P)^U}\right)^{\zeta}$$

$$(3.17)$$

where expected earnings outside the firm are defined as a log-linear combination of expected wage and unemployment benefits, B, weighted by a proxy of the probability of being unemployed and its complement to one, that is the probability of being employed elsewhere and ξ is the elasticity of effort with respect to the ratio of wages over expected earnings.

Equation (3.17) can equivalently be written as:

$$e = \left(\frac{(W/P)^U}{(W^e/W)^{(1-U)}(B/P)^U} \right)^{\zeta} \tag{3.18}$$

Let us now specify the production function simply as:

$$F = A(eNH)^{\alpha}K^{\beta} \tag{3.19}$$

Hence:

$$\frac{\partial F}{\partial e} = \alpha e^{(\alpha-1)}(NH)^{\alpha}K^{\beta} \tag{3.20}$$

and

$$\frac{\partial e}{\partial(W/P)} = \zeta Ue(W/P)^{-1} \tag{3.21}$$

Substituting (3.20) and (3.21) into equation (3.16) yields:

$$\left(\frac{W}{P} \right)^{1-U \cdot \zeta\alpha} = A(NH)^{\alpha}K^{\beta}\alpha\zeta U \left[\left(\frac{W^e}{W} \right)^{1-U} \left(\frac{B}{P} \right)^U \right]^{-\zeta\alpha} \tag{3.22}$$

Since $A(NH)^{\alpha}K^{\beta} = Q = \bar{Q}$, equation (3.22) finally becomes, using logarithms:

$$(w-p)^{EW} = \frac{1}{(1-U\zeta\alpha)}[y^e - \varepsilon(p-p^e) + \ln\alpha + \ln\zeta + \ln U$$
$$+ \zeta\alpha(1-U)(w-w^e) - \zeta\alpha U(b-p)] \tag{3.23}$$

3.2.3 The insider-outsider model

The efficiency wage theory suits a labour market where workers have no bargaining power though they can choose the amount of effort. Such conditions may capture relevant features of the United States labour market but are less representative of the European market where the presence of unions is pervasive.

Models in which single workers or groups of workers play a role in the process of wage determination are based on the theory of insiders-outsiders[8] and on the theory of bargaining between firms and unions.[9] These two approaches can be assimilated for several reasons. First of all, insiders are induced to organize themselves in groups in order to increase the rents they can exploit from their position; thereby they give rise to and justify the existence of unions. Second, as long as membership is allowed to vary in union models, the considerations that can be made for the insiders can be extended to the group of employed union members. For these reasons the wage derived below is based on the insider-outsider model. According to the latter the insiders, whose bargaining power is relatively higher than that of the outsiders because of the costs that the firm has already spent on them, will choose the maximum level of wage which assures that they will remain employed; this level of wage is simply be derived from the labour demand equation (3.13) in which employment N is replaced by the number of insiders N^I; using logarithms:

$$(w-p)^I = -(1+\rho_1)n^I - \ln 1/\alpha + y^e - \xi(h-\bar{h}) - \rho_0 R + \rho_1 l$$
$$- \varepsilon(p-p^e) + (w-w^e) \tag{3.24}$$

The status of insider is decided according to a membership rule, a general specification of which is the following:

$$N^I = N_{-1} + \theta(L-N)_{-1}, 0 \le \theta \le 1 \tag{3.25}$$

that is, the insiders are those employed last year plus a fraction of the unemployed; dividing this equation by θL_{-1} and transforming into logarithms yields:[10]

$$n^I = l_{-1} - \frac{(1-\theta)}{\theta} U_{-1} + \frac{(1-\theta)}{\theta} + \ln(\theta) \tag{3.26}$$

which can be substituted into equation (3.24):

$$(w - p)^I = -(1 + \rho_1)l_{-1} + \frac{(1 - \theta)(1 + \rho_1)}{\theta} U_{-1} + y^e - \xi(h - \bar{h})$$
$$- \rho_0 R - \rho_1 U - \varepsilon \cdot (p - p^e) + (w - w^e) - \ln 1/\alpha$$
$$- \frac{(1 - \theta)(1 + \rho_1)}{\theta} - (1 + \rho_1)\ln(\theta) \qquad (3.27)$$

Finally, the overall wage equation is obtained as a log-linear combination of the three equations derived above:

$$(w - p) = \lambda_1(w - p)^C + \lambda_2(w - p)^{EW} + \lambda_3(w - p)^I \qquad (3.28)$$

By substituting the definitions:

$$(w - p) = c + \left[\frac{\lambda_1}{(\eta(1 + \rho_1) + 1)} + \lambda_3\right](y^e - l) + \frac{\lambda_2}{(1 - U\zeta\alpha)}(y^e)$$
$$- \xi\left[\frac{\lambda_1}{(\eta(1 + \rho_1) + 1)} + \lambda_3\right](h - \bar{h}) + \left[\lambda_3\frac{(1 - \rho_1)(1 - \theta)}{\theta}\right]U_{-1}$$
$$+ \frac{\lambda_2}{(1 - U\zeta\alpha)}\ln U - \rho_0\left[\frac{\lambda_1}{(\eta(1 + \rho_1) + 1)} + \lambda_3\right]R$$
$$+ \frac{\lambda_1}{(\eta + 1/(1 + \rho_1))}\eta(T_1 + T_2) + \frac{\lambda_1}{(\eta + 1/(1 + \rho_1))}\eta\chi(pc - p)$$
$$- \frac{\lambda_2}{(1 - U\zeta\alpha)}U\zeta\alpha(b - p) + \left[\frac{\lambda_1}{(\eta(1 + \rho_1) + 1)}\right.$$
$$\left. + \frac{\lambda_2}{(1 - U\zeta\alpha)}(1 - U)\zeta\alpha + \lambda_3\right](w - w^e)$$
$$- \varepsilon\left[\frac{\lambda_1}{(\eta(1 + \rho_1) + 1)} + \frac{\lambda_2}{(1 - U\zeta\alpha)} + \lambda_3\right](p - p^e)$$
$$\qquad (3.29)$$

where:

$$c = -\left[\frac{\lambda_1}{\eta(1 + \rho_1) + 1} + \lambda_3\right]\ln(1/\alpha) + \frac{\lambda_2}{(1 - U\zeta\alpha)}\ln(\alpha\zeta)$$
$$- \lambda_3\frac{(1 - \theta)(1 - \rho_1)}{\theta} - \lambda_3(1 - \rho_1)\ln(\theta)$$

3.3   A MODEL OF STRIKES

The model of strikes developed below (Cristini, 1989) is based on the concept of the 'relative' wage which typically applies when different groups of workers are present; let subscripts i and j indicate two different groups; then the relative real wage RW is defined as follows:

$$\ln(RW)_{ij} = \ln\left(\frac{\bar{W}}{P_{co}}\right)_i - \ln\left(\frac{\bar{W}}{P_{co}}\right)_j, i \neq j \tag{3.30}$$

where $\bar{W}$ is the after tax nominal wage and P_{co} are consumption prices. An aggregate expression of (3.30) is obtained by summing the upper diagonal elements of the matrix RW_{ij} and then dividing by $(n^2 - n)/2$, where n is the total number of groups:

$$\ln(RW) = \sum_{i>j=1}^{n} \frac{\ln(RW)_{ij}}{(n^2 - n)/2} \tag{3.31}$$

Suppose that the equilibrium wage structure is the one that has become accepted through time; then it may be assumed to be a function of past values of RW_{ij}:

$$\ln(RW)_{ij}^* = \sum_{s=1}^{m} \beta_s \left[\ln\left(\frac{\bar{W}}{P_{co}}\right)_{i,t-s} - \ln\left(\frac{\bar{W}}{P_{co}}\right)_{j,t-s} \right] \tag{3.32}$$

and, in aggregate:

$$\ln(RW)^* = \sum_{i>j=1}^{n} \frac{\ln(RW)^{*ij}}{(n^2 - n)/2} \tag{3.33}$$

The definition given in (3.30) is used by Paldam (1989) according to whom, for any group of workers, the probability of a strike action is a function of the actual wage structure.

Alternatively we argue that strikes are caused by a *change* in the wage structure and act as a corrective mechanism taking *RW* back to *RW**.

Given the difficulty of comparing groups of workers across the OECD, we imagine that the relative wage relevant to the workers is defined with respect to a certain 'aspiration' level and apply the same reasoning as above. Then the tension that may lead to a strike arises whenever the actual consumption wage is below the aspiration consumption wage. More precisely, it is reasonable to assume that strikes, being costly, occur only if the tension is sufficiently strong – if the gap between the actual and the aspired wage is greater than the cost of a strike. Moreover, for a given tension and a given strike cost, the stronger the union the more inclined it will be to pursue the strike in order to secure its members the desired real wage. Formally we have:

$$Prob(NC) = Prob\left[\ln\frac{(\bar{W}/P_{co})^*}{(\bar{W}/P_{co})}\right] > (SC - \omega UP) \qquad (3.34)$$

where *NC* are conflicts, $(\bar{W}/P_{CO})^*$ and $(\bar{W}/P_{CO})$ are aspiration and actual consumption wage respectively, *SC* is the cost of the strike and ωUP reflects the influence of union strength on the final decision. In turn these variables are defined follows:

$$\ln(\bar{W}/P_{co})^* = \ln(W/P)^e + \ln(WE)^e \qquad (3.35)$$

$$\ln(\bar{W}/P_{co}) = \ln(W/P) + \ln(WE) \qquad (3.36)$$

$$SC = \ln(\bar{W}/P_{co}) - \left\{\vartheta\ln(SP) + (1-\vartheta)\left[(1-U)\ln(\bar{W}/P_{co})^*\right.\right.$$
$$\left.\left. + U\ln\left(\frac{B}{P(Pc/P)^\chi}\right)\right]\right\} \qquad (3.37)$$

where *WE* is the wedge as defined in equation 3.11, *SP* is the strike pay, ϑ is the fraction of workers who carry on striking and $\frac{B}{P(Pc/P)^\chi}$ are consumption benefits. Substituting equations (3.35) to (3.37) into equation (3.34) and scaling by the number of employees yields:

$$
\begin{aligned}
NC/N = {} & [1 - (1 - \vartheta)(1 - U)][(T_1 + T_2)^e - (T_1 + T_2)] \\
& + [1 + (1 - \vartheta)(1 - U)]\chi[(pc - p)^e - (pc - p)] \\
& - [1 + (1 - \vartheta)(1 - U)][(w - p) - (w - p)^e] \\
& + \vartheta \ln(SP) + [1 + (1 - \vartheta)(1 - U)](w - p) \\
& + [1 - (1 - \vartheta)(1 - U)](T_1 + T_2) \\
& + \chi\vartheta(pc - p) + (1 - \vartheta)U(b - p) + \omega UP/N
\end{aligned}
$$

$$(3.38)$$

The first three terms are forecasting errors of real variables (the wedge and the product wage); under rational expectations they are innovations and may be safely relegated to the error term. Under different expectational assumptions they are approximated by their current and past changes. It is interesting to replace the real wage by its determinants: the rate of unemployment, the wedge, and the real interest rate. Equation (3.38) makes clear the direct relationship existing between conflicts and union power; since the latter is unobservable, we assume that some of its information is embodied in the lagged number of conflicts which also justifies a dynamic version of (3.38).

3.4   OECD AND LDC AGGREGATE DEMAND

OECD aggregate demand is distinguished into the usual national account components; to facilitate the empirical analysis the system is defined, from the start, in a log-linear form:

$$\ln Y = \alpha_C \ln C + \alpha_I \ln I + \alpha_G \ln G + \alpha_X \ln X - \alpha_M \ln M$$

$$(3.39)$$

where C is consumption, I investments, G public expenditure, X exports and M imports and α's are the elasticities of aggregate demand to the relative component.

Each component is defined in a log linear form according to a standard manner:

$$\alpha_C \ln C = c_0 + c_1(y - T_1) + c_2(m - p) + c_3 R - c_4 \Delta p$$
$$\alpha_I \ln I = i_0 + i_1 \Delta y + i_2(m - p) - i_3 R - i_4 \Delta p + i_5 \Pi^e - i_6 T_2$$
$$\alpha_G \ln G = \alpha_G(g - p)$$
$$\alpha_X \ln X = x_0 + x_1 y^* + x_2(pc - p)$$
$$\alpha_M \ln M = m_0 + m_1 y - m_2(pc - p)$$

$$(3.40)$$

where $m - p$ is real money supply and Π^e are the firms' expected cash flows. Public expenditure is taken as given as it is assumed to be an exogenous policy instrument. As far as the signs of the coefficients are concerned, we recognize that the effect of the real interest rate on private consumption is 'a priori' ambiguous since it rises interests payment on financial wealth but also it rises the burden on debt. Summing the various components and solving for Y we obtain, in logarithms:

$$y = \frac{1}{1 - c_1 - i_1 + m_1}[(c_0 + i_o + x_0 - m_0) + (c_2 + i_2)(m - p)$$
$$+ (c_3 - i_3)R - (c_4 + i_4)\Delta p + i_5 \Pi^e - c_1 T_1 - i_6 T_2$$
$$+ (x_2 + m_2)(pc - p) + x_1 y^* - i_1 y_{-1} + \alpha_G(g - p)]$$

$$(3.41)$$

We may think of an analogous equation holding for the LDC bloc; the variables, in this case, are tagged with a star. Notice that the signs of the coefficients on $(pc - p)$ in the export and import equations will be, however reversed; that is, we expect $m_2^* > 0$ and $x_2^* < 0$.

3.5 THE FINANCIAL MARKET

The real interest rate equation is obtained by equating funds' supply, that is OECD private and public savings plus LDC trade surpluses, and funds' demand that is OECD private and public investments plus LDC trade deficits. Using the nationa account definitions given above we obtain:

$$
\begin{aligned}
y - c_0 - c_1(y - T_1) &- c_2(m - p) - c_3 R + c_4 \Delta p + \bar{x}_0 + \bar{x}_1 y \\
&- \bar{x}_2(pc - p) - \bar{m}_0 - \bar{m}_1 \bar{y} - \bar{m}_2(pc - p) = i_0 + i_1 \Delta y \\
&+ i_2(m - p) - i_3 R - i_4 \Delta p + i_5 \Pi^e - i_6 T_2 + \alpha_G(g - p) \\
&+ \hat{m}_0 + \hat{m}_1 \hat{y} + \hat{m}_2(pc - p) - \hat{x}_0 - \hat{x}_1 y + \hat{x}_2(pc - p)
\end{aligned}
$$

(3.42

where a bar indicates LDC surplus economies (mainly oi exporting countries) and a hat indicates LDC economies in trade deficit (mainly oil importing countries). Solving for R we obtain

$$
\begin{aligned}
R = \frac{1}{(c_3 - i_3)} &(-c_0 - i_0 + x_0^* - m_0^*) + (c_1 + x_1^*)y + i_1 \Delta y - c_1 T_1 \\
&+ i_6 T_2 - (c_2 + i_2)(m - p) - (c_4 + i_4)\Delta p - (x_2^* + m_2^*)(pc - p) \\
&- \bar{m}_1 \bar{y} - \hat{m}_1 \hat{y} - i_5 \Pi^e - \alpha_G(g - p)
\end{aligned}
$$

(3.43

where a star indicates the whole of LDC countries given by the sum of trade surplus and trade deficit economies.[11] A: explained in the previous chapter the actual working of the world capital market is conditioned on past developments o. financial funds' demand and supply. The real interest rate equation is therefore extended to comprise the level of LDC external debt and the level of OECD government debt. The lag structure of the equation is chosen empirically. Notice that the signs of the coefficients are actually ambiguous depending or the sign and size of R in the consumption function.

In order to obtain an equation describing the evolution of LDC external debt over time, we start by the time derivative of the real level of debt:

$$
\frac{\partial(S/P)}{\partial t} = \frac{\frac{\partial S}{\partial t} P - \frac{\partial P}{\partial t} S}{P^2} = \frac{\partial S}{\partial t} \frac{1}{P} - \frac{\partial P}{\partial t} \frac{S}{P} = M^* - X^* + i \frac{S_{-1}}{P} - A - \Delta p \frac{S}{P}
$$

(3.44

where the evolution of the level of debt is split into the real trade component $(M - X)$, the interest payment on past debt (iS_{-1}/P) and financial aid from the North (A), in real terms;[12] dividing both sides by $(S/P)_{-1}$ we obtain approximately:

$$\frac{\partial(S/P)/\partial t}{(S/P)_{-1}} = \frac{M^* - X^* - A}{(S/P)_{-1}} + (i - \Delta p) \tag{3.45}$$

where $i - \Delta p$ is the real interest rate. In order to have an empirically tractable equation we use a log-linear approximation to the above expression:

$$\Delta(s - p) = \ln M^* - \ln X^* - \ln A - \ln(S/P)_{-1} + R \tag{3.46}$$

Imports and exports have been already defined, in logarithmic form, in the aggregate demand; financial aid from the North is assumed to be a log-linear function of OECD economic activity, of the real interest rate and of the level of existing debt:

$$\ln A = a_0 - a_1 R - a_2(s - p) + a_3 y \tag{3.47}$$

Substituting for $\ln M^*$, $\ln X^*$ and $\ln A$ we obtain:

$$\begin{aligned} \Delta(s - p) = {} & (m_0 - x_0 - a_0) + (m_2 + x_2)(pc - p) - (x_1 + a_3)y \\ & + (1 + a_1)R + (a_2 - 1)(s - p)_{-1} + m_1 y^* \end{aligned}$$

which may be re-arranged as:

$$\begin{aligned} (s - p) = {} & a_2(s - p)_{-1} + (m_0 - x_0 - a_0) + (m_2 + x_2)(pc - p) \\ & - (x_1 + a_3)y + (1 + a_1)R + m_1 y^* \end{aligned} \tag{3.48}$$

3.6   THE PRIMARY COMMODITY MARKET

The usual reduced form aggregated primary commodity price equation is determined (Gilbert, 1988, 1989b) from the market clearing condition according to which:

$$Q_c + F_{-1} = C_c + F \tag{3.49}$$

that is production of commodity (Q_c) plus past storage (F_{-1}) equals demand (C_c) plus present stockholding demand (F). This equilibrium condition, which holds at any point in time, simplifies, in the long-run, to the equality between production and demand since storage will be constant.

The introduction of stockholding requires a special attention as the optimal inventory condition may be specified in two alternative ways (Deaton and Laroque, 1990). In one case stockholdings are assumed to be non-negative: when the expected capital gain is negative they are zero; when they are positive the expected capital gain is zero due to arbitrage. This is represented by the following complementary slackness condition:[13]

$$F_t \geq 0 : (1 - \delta)pc_{t+1|t} \leq pc_t + i_t + c_t \qquad (3.50)$$

where pc is the log of commodity price, i is the interest rate, c is the log of storage costs, δ is the deterioration factor and subscript $t + 1|t$ indicates expectations of $t + 1$ formed at t.

In a second case the non-negativity constraint is not imposed; stocks are simply a function of the expected capital gain (Muth, 1961):

$$F_t = \alpha[(1 - \delta)pc_{t+1|t} - pc_t - i_t - c_t] \qquad (3.51)$$

where $\alpha = \dfrac{1}{A[(pc_{t+1} - pc_{t+1|t})^2]^e}$ and A is a measure of risk aversion.

This second case reverts to the first one if risk neutrality is approached or if the risk can be completely diversified or offset in efficient future markets, as long as $F > 0$. The non-linearity implicit in the first function originates from the non-negativity constraint; the importance of the latter is clear for some agricultural products which are not carried over from one harvest to the next and indeed the argument for non-linearity traces back to Gustafson (1958) who was concerned with agricultural crops. The same argument however applies to non-agricultural commodities as long as storage costs are not negligible. For these non-storable commodities stocks build up only after a positive supply or a negative demand shock thereby allowing the price to fall sufficiently for a rational investor to hold stocks (in view of a future capital gain). On the contrary stocks cannot go below zero in the aftermath of a negative supply or a positive demand shock and the commodity price must bear all the burden of the adjustment. Hence the commodity price response to equal but opposite shocks is asymmetric, with high sharp rises and long downs.[14]

The linear function, on the other hand, implies an identical intensity of the commodity price response to either excess demand or supply. Nevertheless, for facility in modelling and estimation, it is usual practice to define linear storage functions.[15] This choice is less controversial for an aggregated commodity index; indeed for many commodities (for example minerals and metals) warehousing costs and deterioration are negligible and production is a continuous process rather than a discrete one. In addition harvest seasons differ across products and convenience yield may be important so that it is acceptable to assume that, in aggregate, some stocks are always held.

Following Gilbert (1988) the primary commodity production and demand are assumed to be a function of the logarithm of the price pc:

$$Q_{ct} = \bar{Q}_{ct}(1 + \sigma_{1t} + \epsilon(pc_t - \overline{pc}_t))$$
$$C_{ct} = \bar{C}_{ct}(1 + \sigma_{2t} + e(pc_t - \overline{pc}_t)) \tag{3.52}$$

where σ_1 and σ_2 are price independent deviations of production and demand from normal, ε and e are elasticities and a bar indicates normal values. By substituting the production and consumption function, normalized to their trend values, into the equilibrium condition (3.49) above we obtain:

$$\Delta F_t = (\epsilon + e)(pc - \overline{pc}) + (\sigma_1 - \sigma_2) \tag{3.53}$$

Using this expression together with the linear stock demand function (3.51) a second order difference equation in F_t is obtained. As shown in Pesaran (1987) and Gilbert and Palaskas (1990) this equation can equivalently be expressed in terms of the commodity price; the latter is a useful specification in our case since stock data on total commodities cannot be used. The reduced form commodity price equation then looks as follows:

$$pc_t = \mu(pc_{t-1} + i_{t-1}) + (1 - \mu)/(\epsilon + e) \sum_{i=0}^{\infty} \mu^i(\sigma_{t+i|t} - \mu\sigma_{t+i|t-i})$$

$$- \mu \sum_{i=0}^{\infty} \mu^i(i_{t+i|t} - \mu i_{t+i|t-i}) \qquad (3.54)$$

where μ is the stable root from the second order difference equation.

This basic specification can be extended in several important ways.

1. Production and consumption can, more realistically, be made dependent on past expectations of current prices, thereby extending the lag structure (Pesaran, 1987, Gilbert and Palaskas, 1990).
2. Changes in the values of the currency in which the commodity price is denominated may affect the commodity price itself (Gilbert 1989a, 1990a). Using a single commodity model based on demand and supply Ridler and Yandle (1972) demonstrated that a 100 per cent appreciation of the dollar, the currency at which commodities are usually denominated, determines a 100 $(1 - v_{1j})$ per cent fall of the dollar denominated primary commodity price where v_{1j} are the elasticity-weighted shares of US production and consumption of the commodity (Gilbert, 1989a).[16] Extension to a multi-commodity framework (Chambers and Just 1979, Gilbert, 1990a) showed that the elasticity of the commodity price to the exchange rate appreciation is still between 0 and 1. Further extensions to a model comprising stockholding (Gilbert, 1990a) do not invalidate the above results. However, in empirical works, the elasticity of the dollar-denominated commodity price to a dollar appreciation typically exceeds unity; Gilbert (1989a) provides two explanations for this fact, one related to the exchange rate used in the estimation and the other one related to LDC

indebtedness. The latter explanation puts forward a further link between primary commodity prices and LDC external debt the causality of which runs from LDC external debt to primary commodity prices. As explained in the previous chapter, the presence of LDC external debt as a regressor in the primary commodity price equation can also capture the surge of commodity supply induced by the necessity to serve growing interest payments.

3. The above equation is derived for a representative storable commodity which is traded in efficient markets. However, in defining an aggregated commodity price it is reasonable to adopt a looser specification[17] in particular:

   a) Restrictions on the coefficients are not imposed a priori and a looser lag structure is initially introduced.

   b) Future demand and supply imbalances are not derived from a structural demand and supply model but are replaced by proxies of expected demand and supply.

   c) The use of an error correction specification is suggested on several grounds: i) it can appropriately represent forward looking expectations when exogenous variables follow an IMA process; ii) commodity prices tend to move in line with other prices; iii) the relevant commodity price may be the nominal one in the short one and the real one in the long run. At this regard Gilbert (1989a) finds that is fundamentally incorrect to specify short-run primary commodity price equations in real terms and we arrived to an analogous conclusion in Chapter 1.

4. Recent estimations (Gilbert, 1989a) find more satisfactory results when using backward looking expectations in ECM than when using forward-looking models.

The commodity price equation, specified according to an ECM therefore looks as follows:

$$\Delta pn_t = a_0 + L(a_{1j}\Delta pn_{t-j}) + L(a_{2j}\Delta \iota_{t-j}) + L(a_{3j}\Delta \sigma_{t-j})$$
$$+ L(a_{4j}\Delta \delta_{t-j}) + \{a_5(pn-p)_{t-1} + a_6 R_{t-1}$$
$$+ a_7 \bar{\sigma}_{t-1} + a_8 \bar{\delta}_{t-1}\} \tag{3.55}$$

where L indicates distributed lags, *pn* is the aggregate index price of non-oil primary commodities expressed in OECD currency, i is the nominal interest rate, σ and δ are the logarithms of supply and demand indicators which may originate both from the North and from the South. The term in curly brackets is the error correction term: as it represents the long run relationship, variables are here in real terms. The lag structure of the equation is chosen empirically. The vector of demand and supply imbalances we take to include present and past values of the following variables: the price of oil, the OECD rate of unemployment, the LDC external debt.

4 Estimations and Simulations

The model is estimated by Three Stages Least Squares adopting the 'general to specific' methodology according to which the final parsimonious estimate is obtained from an initial unrestricted over-parametrized system (Hendry, 1989; Hendry and Richard, 1983).

In order to obtain an empirically tractable model, the following approximations are used: in the price and wage equations ($y^e - l$) is proxied by ($yt - l$) where yt is trend GDP as defined in the data section at the end of the book; price (wage) forecasting errors are defined as the residuals of an AR(3) price (wage) inflation equation which imposes long-run neutrality (see data section). The estimated model is reported in the appendix to this chapter; for each equation the steady-state solution is also computed and presented.

In the next four sections we will briefly comment on the single equation estimates; the functioning of the overall estimated model is discussed from Section 4.5.

4.1 THE ESTIMATED OECD SUPPLY SIDE

The estimated *production function* indicates decreasing returns to scale and no significant impact of deviations of working hours from trend. The long-run elasticities of output with respect to employment and capital are 0.37 and 0.41 respectively.

In the *price equation* both the real rate of interest and the rate of unemployment are statistically significant.

According to the theories reviewed in the previous chapter, the presence of the real interest rate suggests a variable mark-up. In particular, as long as the real interest rate captures the

87

value that the firm attaches to the future, its positive impact, both in the short-run, in terms of ΔR, as well as in the long run, gives credit to the customer market model rather than to the implicit collusion hypothesis. The level of aggregation, however, prevents us from being conclusive on this issue.

The rate of unemployment, which captures both cyclical changes of the marginal cost as well as additional cyclical movements of the mark-up affecting the elasticity of demand, shows a negative coefficient. Since the latter exceeds unity, in the long run, we are inclined to think that the elasticity of demand is counter-cyclical, that is it is a positive function of U. The value of the coefficient implies that, in the long-run, a 1 percentage point (p.p.) rise of the rate of unemployment determines a 3.3 per cent fall of the price mark-up over wages.

In order to investigate if primary commodity prices are a further indicator of the cycle, they were added as regressors in the price mark-up equation but both the oil and non-oil component showed insignificant (negative) coefficients.

Finally, unexpected changes in wages, that is wage forecasting errors, are significant and determine, as expected, a decline of the price-mark up over wages.

As far as the *labour market* is concerned a few results stand out in the wage equation:[1]

1. industrial conflicts have a marked effect;
2. the positive coefficient of the lagged unemployment rate suggests the existence of some insider power;
3. the real interest rate appears with a significant negative coefficient;
4. the wedge effect is captured by the aggregated commodity price index but there is no explicit resistance to taxes; the latter are introduced via industrial strikes;
5. a time trend, theoretically linked to trend GDP, is also significant.

The importance of conflicts as a proxy of union power is evident once conflicts are substituted out using the relevant equation: unions reinforce wage resistance not only by more than tripling the long-run real wage elasticity to non-oil primary commodity prices, which becomes 0.036 (having considered the average value of the share of imports), but also by introducing a reaction to tax increases. Moreover industrial conflicts are found, as usual, to be strongly pro-cyclical and indeed revolve the sign of the coefficient of the rate of unemployment: once conflicts are substituted out, a 1 p.p. rise of the rate of unemployment induces, in the long-run, a 0.25 per cent fall of the real wage. The fact that real wages respond to the rate of unemployment implies that a recession in the North can dampen OECD inflation directly, that is even in absence of a recession-induced fall of primary commodity prices. On the contrary Beckerman and Jenkinson (1986) sustain that the fall of OECD inflation in the early eighties is explained by the decline of primary commodity prices which, being absent an OECD Phillips curve, were indeed the only prices responding to the OECD recession. For a critical view on this point see also Gilbert (1990a).

The results of the VAR analysis performed in the first chapter as well as the theoretical considerations discussed in Chapter 3, suggested distinguishing between the oil and the non-oil components of the overall primary commodity price index.[2] Along these lines $(pn - p)$ and $(po - p)$ were separately included both in the wage and in the number of conflicts equation.

In the conflicts equation the non-oil component was the only one close to significance (coeff = 0.115, 't' 1.38) and this latter result was confirmed by the equation standard error which was lower when including the non-oil price index than when including the aggregate index. On the contrary, the oil price index at date t was the only commodity price component slightly significant in the wage equation (coeff. = 0.0499, 't' = 1.38); however this result was not corroborated by the standard error of the equation which indicated, instead, a relevant information carried by the aggregated commodity price index[3] which was finally retained in the equation.

The presence of the real interest rate, with a long-run elasticity of -0.63, is consistent with its presence in the price mark-up equation; moreover, since the real rate of interest enters via the insider model and the competitive one, its presence substantiates the relevance of these two wage formation mechanisms.

The coefficient on price forecasting errors is rather low perhaps because of wage-indexation mechanisms.

The *labour force* equation is fundamentally explained by a time trend although in the short-run, positive changes in the expected real wage are also significant.

As explained in Chapter 2 the *OECD rate of unemployment* is also determined within the OECD supply side. In the short-run it is simply defined by the identity $U = l - n$, where n is obtained by inverting the production function; in the long-run it is derived, together with real wage, by solving the wage-price system. In this case, once the number of conflicts are substituted out, the steady-state rate of unemployment is given by the following expression:

$$U = -0.6914 - 0.0772(yt - l) + 0.12966T + 0.003094(po - p)$$
$$+ 0.01025(pn - p) + 0.00287t - 0.03095R$$

$$(4.1)$$

where χ and α have been replaced by their sample average values.

Expression (4.1) shows two unusual variables for a long-run unemployment equation: the first one is trend productivity, defined as the ratio between trend output and the labour force; trend productivity does not usually enter the rate of unemployment expression as it is constrained to enter the price and wage equation with equal value and opposite sign; this restriction however is not accepted by our data hence not imposed. The productivity effect is counterbalanced by the positive trend effect.

The second variable which is worthwhile discussing is the real interest rate whose coefficient is negative, although small, both when conditioning on non-oil prices, as in equation (4.1) as well as when substituting them out using their relevant long-run expression:

$$U = -0.6057 - 0.07283(yt - l) + 0.1194T + 0.00449(po - p)$$
$$+ 0.00138(k - l) - 0.00288k - 0.00257a + 0.002678t$$
$$- 0.038168R + 0.00231dum$$

(4.2)

As discussed in the Chapter 3, the effect of the real interest rate on the rate of unemployment is the compound result of two opposite forces since the presence of R in (4.2) is due to the presence of R both in the price and in the wage equation.[4]

Other empirical studies concerned with the effects of the real interest rate on the rate of unemployment found mixed results. Phelps (1994), using a panel of 17 OECD countries from 1957 to 1989, finds that the world short-term real interest rate has a positive impact on the national rates of unemployment. Manning (1991), by estimating a dynamic wage-setting equation for 19 OECD countries from 1956 to 1985, finds that the real interest rate is significant in only 10 countries and for 9 of these the relationship with the rate of unemployment is positive. Bean (1994) finds that the time-specific fixed-effect obtained by estimating a model of the rate of unemployment for 20 OECD countries from 1956 to 1992, is negatively correlated with the G7 short-term real interest rate.

An interpretation of these inconsistent results in terms of the interplay of two conflicting pressures seems to go some way towards an explanation.

4.2 OECD AND LDC ESTIMATED AGGREGATE DEMAND

OECD aggregate demand is positively affected by real money balances and growth of LDC GDP whereas it is depressed by a high level of inflation and, even more, by a growing rate of inflation. Empirically the potential effect of the South on the

North aggregate demand, working via the price of primary commodities,[5] does not show up. Similarly, additional quantity variables, like government spending and taxes, are insignificant. In the long run, demand is driven by real money balances with an elasticity of 0.85.

LDC demand could be estimated only in terms of deviations from trend; it is driven by primary commodity prices and by the state of the OECD economy captured by short-run deviations of GDP from trend and by the rate of unemployment; the impact of the latter impinges into the long-run with an elasticity of −0.6.

As the LDC bloc includes oil-exporting and oil-importing countries, the real prices of oil and non-oil primaries, separately introduced, approximate the terms of trade of the two groups of countries: it turns out that improvements in the terms of trade of the oil-exporting countries are beneficial for the LDC GDP on the whole whereas real non-oil primary commodity prices play a less significant role and appear with a negative sign.

4.3 THE ESTIMATED FINANCIAL MARKET

One explanation of the negative impact of real non-oil commodity prices on LDC GDP emerges from the *LDC external debt* equation since, as expected, external debt grows in response to increasing primary commodity prices. In fact both components of primary prices deteriorate LDC external debt but a rise in the price of non-oil primaries produces a larger effect than the rise of oil, the two long-run elasticities being respectively 0.71 and 0.17.

In shaping LDC external debt a substantial role is played by the real interest rate whose 1 p.p. increase raises LDC debt by 2.2 per cent in the short-run and by 5.8 per cent in the long-run.

Both the level and the rate of growth of OECD GDP positively affects LDC external debt with a long-run elasticity of 2.4 per cent; according to the theoretical evolution of debt proposed in Chapter 3, when the OECD economy is buoyant LDC external debt should decline thanks to a debt reimbursement

ɔhase facilitated both by financial aid and by higher exports to
:he North. However the positive sign suggests that an
ɔxpansionary North not only may reduce the cost of borrowing
ɔut may also permit an increase of the number of liabilities
issued to the South, thereby more than counterbalancing the
reimbursement effect on LDC external debt.[6]

LDC external debt and OECD government debt are
important factors in explaining the path of the *real interest
rate*; both debts are expressed in real terms and normalized to
trend GDPs. Indeed these two ratios are the only long-run
determinants of the real interest rate with an elasticity of 0.062
for LDC debt and 0.046 for OECD debt.

In the short-run the real interest rate is also affected by the
growth of real money supply, of OECD GDP and of the rate
of unemployment. If the rate of unemployment is indicative of
the status of private hoardings and hence of the funds supply,
the positive coefficient is expected; likewise GDP growth, if
linked to investment demand through the accelerator,
captures the demand of funds and its positive coefficient is
reasonable.

Our findings about the determinants of the real interest rate
essentially support those of other studies. In particular a
significant role of world debt, either in aggregate, as in Phelps
(1994) or distinguished into the LDC and the industrialized
country components, as in Beenstock (1988), is usually
observed. An exception is Barro and Sala-i-Martin (1990)
who cannot refuse the Ricardian view. Monetary effects,
specified as changes of money supply, as in Barro and Sala-i-
Martin (1990), or as changes in inflation, as in Phelps (1994),
or, again, as the level of money supply as in Beenstock (1988)
usually appear with a significant negative sign. On the other
hand, government budget deficits are normally insignificant
and this was also the case in our estimates. Corroborating
previous results (Barro and Sala-i-Martin, 1990, Phelps, 1994),
changes in the real price of oil were also found to have a
significant and positive sign; however since the diagnostic of
the equation deteriorated considerably, we preferred not to
introduce them.

4.4   THE ESTIMATED PRIMARY COMMODITY MARKET

In the estimated primary commodity equation the rate of OECD unemployment is significant both in differences and in levels. A 1 p.p. increase of the rate of unemployment determines, in the short-run a fall of the nominal price equal to 4.6 per cent and, in the long-run, a fall of the real price equal to 6.7 per cent. A similar value of the long-run elasticity is found by Beenstock (1988) who, by using OECD GDP instead of U, reports an elasticity of 2.55 per cent. By concentrating on a shorter and more recent span the estimated elasticity is usually larger: from 1970 to 1984 Van Wjinbergen (1985) finds a long-run elasticity close to 15 per cent; from 1970 to 1979 a long-run elasticity of real non-oil primary prices to industrial activity equal to 4.3 per cent is also found by Enoch and Panic (1981).

Corroborating initial results by Gilbert (1989a) we also find a significant negative effect of the real LDC external debt: high levels of debts induce, on the part of the indebted countries, a devaluation policy in order to favour exports. Through this channel the real interest rate has an indirect negative effect on non-oil prices; a direct effect, which we would expect also to be negative, is not present in the long-run.[7]

The potential effect of the real interest rate would give credit to the existence of some degree of substitutability between primary commodities and standard financial assets. Then, in response to a rise of the interest rate, the price of commodities would fall as their demand would decline in favour of other financial activities. However, since substitutability between paper assets and commodities is not perfect, it is not clear to which interest rate primary commodity prices would actually respond. As long as storable primary commodities are used as hedge-assets their demand, and hence their price, may increase in periods of uncertainty; this is congruous with the positive coefficient on the spread between the long- and the short-term nominal interest rate which is found statistically significant in the equation.

The positive link with the price of oil, both in short- and in the long-run is an usual result and confirms that commodities are energy intensive; it may also be the case that LDC labour cost is related to the price of oil but such a hypothesis is not explicitly investigated here.

4.5   HOW WE USE THE ESTIMATED MODEL

The next two sections track the theoretical analysis of Chapter 2 and deal with the following topics:[8]

1. the long-run equilibrium solution;
2. the short-run factors and their importance for price expectations and hysteresis in the rate of unemployment.

The final section discusses the results of oil price shock simulations.

4.6   THE LONG-RUN EQUILIBRIUM

The long-run is the reduced form of the steady-state model. In order to explain how it is actually realized we proceed by steps using the graphical analysis introduced in Chapter 2.

Equilibrium in the OECD, conditional on external markets, is obtained by equating the estimated real wage to the price mark-up over wages. The estimated price and wage lines, depicted in the $U - (w - p)$ space are presented in Figure 4.1:[9] their intersection determines the sample average equilibrium real wage and equilibrium rate of unemployment (equal to 5.45 per cent). The rate of unemployment, together with the equilibrium labour supply yields the equilibrium level of employment so that the production function gives the corresponding equilibrium GDP; the OECD demand equation then determines the level of real money necessary to sustain such an equilibrium position. Production function and aggregate demand are depicted in Figure 4.2.

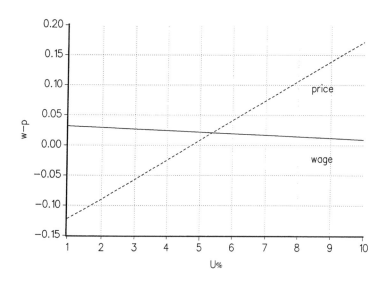

Figure 4.1   Wage and price lines

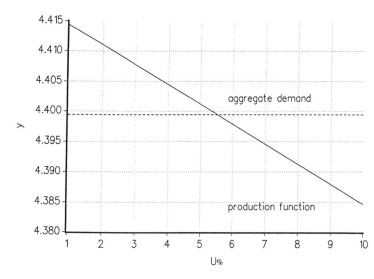

Figure 4.2   Production function and aggregate demand

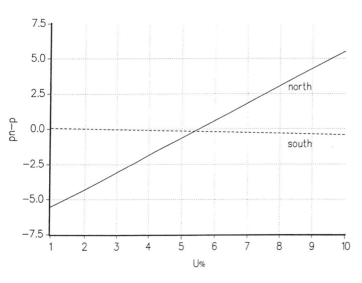

Figure 4.3 North and South lines

In the $U - (pn - p)$ space, the North equilibrium is described, for any equilibrium real wage, by solving $(pn - p)$ as a function of U, after substituting for the financial market equilibrium. The resulting line, which we called North line, is represented in Figure 4.3: it is positively sloped which implies that, for the real wage to be compatible with the price mark-up over wages, that is for inflation to be constant, a rise of primary commodity prices must be accompanied by a rise of the rate of unemployment. In the same $U - (pn - p)$ space the primary commodity market equilibrium, which we called the South line, is represented by a downward sloping line; in the latter LDC external debt has been already replaced by its equilibrium expression. In the sample period considered, the South line is relatively flat which means that in the long-run non-oil commodities are quite elastic to OECD economic activity measured by the rate of unemployment.

In the same space, the financial market equilibrium would be an upward sloping line that is for the real interest rate and LDC external debt to remain in equilibrium, a change in U must be accompanied by a change in the same direction of $pn - p$.

In order to throw some light on the role of the financial market it is instructive to compare the unconditional North and the South lines, that we have just drawn, with the North and South lines conditional on the financial market (that is conditional on the real interest rate and LDC external debt). The slope of the conditional North line is less steep than the slope of the unconditional line (the line rotates downwards around the equilibrium point) implying that the impact of non-oil commodity price shocks on the rate of unemployment is slightly increased.[10] On the contrary, the slope of the conditional South line is steeper than the slope of the unconditional line implying that the impact of OECD demand shocks on non-oil commodity prices is strengthened.

The functioning of the financial market then appears to activate, in the presence of particular shocks, a long-run absorbtion effect which is beneficial for either of the two markets, according to the type of shock. Given the limited bearing of the real interest rate on the steady state OECD rate of unemployment these effects should be relatively more significant for the commodity market than for the OECD economy.

This finding will be further examined on the basis of the simulation results.

Figures 4.4 to 4.11 compare the actual developments of the endogenous variables with their long-run, low frequency paths.[11]

For most of the period the OECD unemployment rate has been below its equilibrium value which shows a rising trend until the mid-1980s and a reversal in direction thereafter. The divergence of the actual value from the equilibrium is widest from the mid-1960s to the early 1970s, ranging between 1 and 2 p.p.; from 1975 the gap reduces as the rate of unemployment undergoes its first jump related to the oil shock. Subsequently, following the second oil crisis, the actual rate of unemployment rises further and in the early 1980s exceeds its equilibrium path; the gap closes towards the end of the sample.

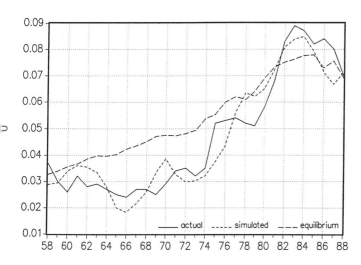

Figure 4.4   OECD rate of unemployment

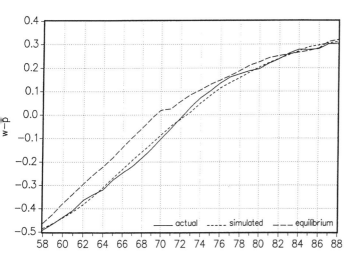

Figure 4.5   Real wage

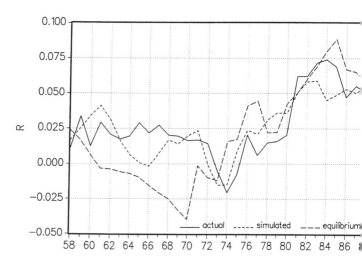

Figure 4.6   Real interest rate

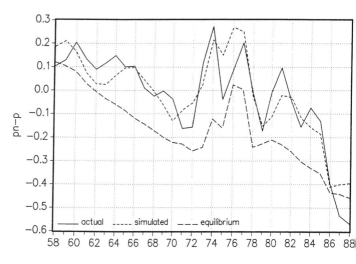

Figure 4.7a   Real non-oil primary commodity price

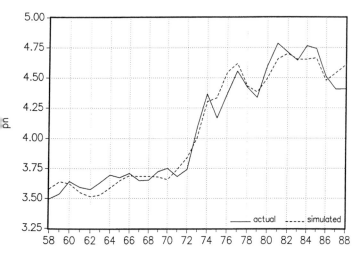

Figure 4.7b Nominal non-oil primary commodity price

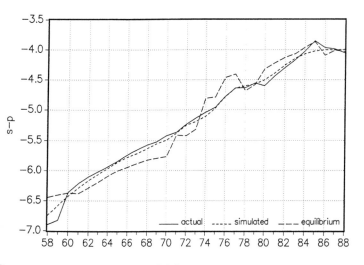

Figure 4.8a Real LDC external debt

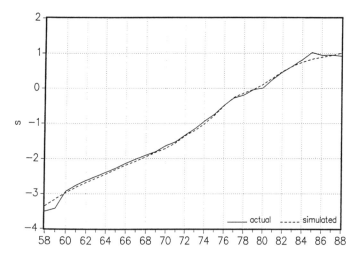

Figure 4.8b   Nominal LDC external debt

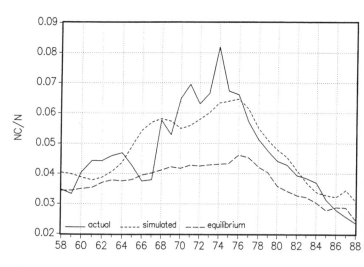

Figure 4.9a   Normalized number of conflicts

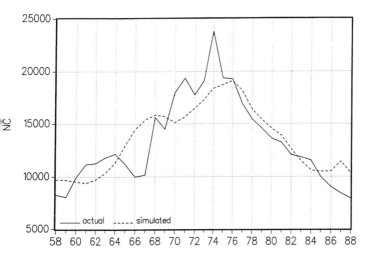

Figure 4.9b Number of conflicts

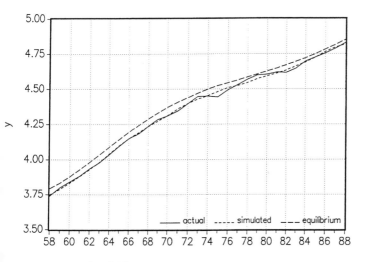

Figure 4.10 OECD GDP

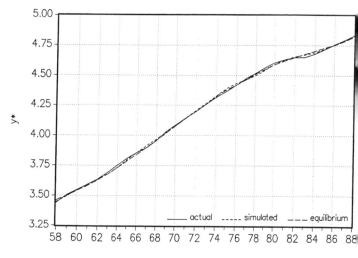

Figure 4.11   LDC GDP

The lower than equilibrium rate of unemployment, which lasted until the mid-1970s, forced the real wage to stay, until then, below its equilibrium; implying that firms managed to remain on their price–employment (or labour demand) equation whereas workers were off their wage (or labour supply) curve. The path of real interest rate which, until the early 1970s, remained above its equilibrium value reinforced this tendency which was only partially counterbalanced by the developments of industrial conflicts and real primary commodity prices, both above their equilibrium paths. After 1976 the gap between actual and equilibrium real wages virtually disappears both because the rate of unemployment comes closer to its equilibrium value and because from the early 1970s to the early 1980s the real interest falls below its long-run value.

Indeed the equilibrium real interest rate shows a declining path below the actual one until 1970; thereafter it starts creeping up and, on average, it is above the actual value; from 1985 the equilibrium value reverts its trend but still exceeds the actual rate.

Until 1986 real primary commodity prices keep above their long-run level; again this is consistent with the path of the actual rate of unemployment which essentially governs commodity demand. Notice that the consistent fall which non-oil primary prices undergo in 1986 determines a drop of the actual path below the equilibrium one.

4.7 THE BREAKDOWN OF THE EQUILIBRIUM PATHS

Using the reduced form of the estimated steady-state system, reported in Table 4.1, it is interesting to break-down the change of the equilibrium endogenous variables into their exogenous determinants.

For this analysis the sample period is divided into five spells. The first one, from 1958 to 1967, is characterized by a relative stability of the variables; the second one, from 1968 to 1973, witnesses the tensions that will lead to the first oil shock; the successive two sub-periods, from 1974 to 1979 and from 1980

Table 4.1 Long-run equilibrium estimated equations

Regressors	U	$pn - p$	R	$w - p$	y^*	$s - p$
		Dependent variables				
c	−0.5696	9.0283	−0.9499	6.9162	0.1879	−31.8636
$yt - l$	−0.0741	0.4011	0.0342	0.7521	0.0368	0.5529
$k - l$	0.0042	0.1868	−0.0743	0.0571	−0.0070	−1.2023
k	−0.0088	−0.3912	0.1556	−0.1196	0.0147	2.5181
a	−0.0079	−0.3493	0.1390	−0.1068	0.0131	2.2489
t	0.0027	−0.0149	−0.0013	0.0097	−0.0014	−0.0205
yt^*	0.0035	0.0653	−0.0925	0.0655	0.9963	−0.4976
T	0.1246	−0.6749	−0.0575	0.4408	−0.0620	−0.9304
$e - p - yt$	−0.0026	−0.0489	0.0693	−0.0491	0.0028	0.3728
dum	0.0018	0.2154	0.0147	−0.0029	−0.0061	0.2385
$po - p$	0.0036	0.1191	0.0243	−0.0025	0.0107	0.3933

Note: variable definition in the data appendix

Table 4.2   Changes of endogenous and exogenous variables by
sub-periods

	58–67 to 68–73	68–73 to 74–79	74–79 to 80–84	80–84 to 85–88
U	0.00174	0.01685	0.03019	0.00206
R	−0.00432	−0.01325	0.05441	−0.00345
$w-p$	0.25616	0.22498	0.11462	0.05206
NC/N	0.02079	0.00093	−0.02219	−0.01318
y	0.34980	0.19230	0.13290	0.13580
y^*	0.40940	0.33400	0.22840	0.13170
$m-p$	0.39818	0.22435	0.12036	0.21279
$e-p$	−0.28300	0.34230	0.51110	0.29260
$e-p-yt$	−0.61510	0.15920	0.34750	0.18350
$s-p$	0.73500	0.60630	0.51190	0.34090
$s-p-yt^*$	0.33620	0.28760	0.25518	0.21010
T	0.05770	0.04827	0.03884	0.00135
Δp	0.02400	0.03518	−0.02109	−0.03235
$pn-p$	−0.19046	0.14172	−0.10319	−0.36928
$po-p$	−0.21260	1.11796	0.76287	−0.62129
po	0.06780	1.59550	1.23790	−0.43580
pn	0.15100	0.59700	0.33300	−0.18400
$k-l$	0.30400	0.20600	0.13000	0.08800
$yt-l$	0.24820	0.12360	0.06250	0.05390
k	0.37100	0.28900	0.22500	0.14300
a	0.24852	0.05173	0.02566	0.06749
l	0.08500	0.08000	0.07900	0.05500
yt^*	0.41730	0.32810	0.22890	0.13070

Note: variable definition in the data appendix

to 1984, are those incorporating the two oil crisis whereas the
last one, from 1985 to 1988, sees falling commodity prices
associated with a reduction of the rate of unemployment and of
the real interest rate. Table 4.2 reports the actual changes of
the endogenous and exogenous variables between these
periods.

4.7.1   The economic situation in the five sub-periods

From the first to the second period a few notable pressures initiate a period of strain and instability: industrial conflicts per employee rise by 2 per cent in response to a 6 p.p. increase of the tax rates, inflation rises by 2.3 per cent and real wages grow by 26 per cent; in real terms oil and non-oil prices are still falling though, between the two periods, the nominal oil price rises by 7 per cent and non-oil prices by 15 per cent. Real money supply rises by 40 per cent whereas OECD government debt falls in real terms and even more with respect to trend GDP; trend productivity is still growing at a high pace (24 per cent) and so is the capital/labour force ratio (30 per cent); like-wise GDP rises by 35 per cent in the OECD and by 41 per cent in the LDC which also increase their external debt by 73 per cent; the latter is also rising relative to trend GDP.

The situation in the early 1970s determined a brisk transformation of this picture. From the period 1968–73 to the next one, 1974–79, the real price of oil rises by 112 per cent and that of non-oil prises by 14 per cent, the growth of trend productivity halves to 12 per cent and that of the capital/labour force ratio falls to 21 per cent. The real interest rate reduces by 1.3 p.p. as the dollar devalued after its inconvertibility was declared; inflation starts rising and OECD GDP growth reduces to 19 per cent while the rate of unemployment rises by almost 2 p.p.; OECD governments implement stricter monetary policies but start enlarging their debts. In the meantime LDC external debt rises by 61 per cent.

From the third to the fourth period – from the second half if the 1970s to the first half of the 1980s the overall situation worsens further: although the increase in the real price of oil attenuates and real non-oil commodity prices start falling, the growth of trend productivity halves again (0.06 per cent) and the capital/labour force ratio falls to (8.8 per cent). Real money supply appears still tighter, rising only by 12 per cent between the third period and the next one; consequently the real interest rate undergoes a sharp rise and increases by 5.4 p.p., regardless of the decline in inflation. OECD government debt rises by 51 per cent in real terms and by 34 per cent with respect to trend GDP. The rate of unemployment grows by 3 p.p., GDP growth declines from 19 per cent to 13 per cent in the OECD and from 33 per cent to 22 per cent in the LDC.

During the final part of the 1980s, from 1980–84 to 1985–88, monetary policy gets looser and a control of public debt seems under way; inflation keeps falling at a pace even higher than before (–3.2 per cent), the rise of the OECD unemployment rate weakens and the change of the rate of interest becomes negative. Moreover, although the rate of growth of the capital/labour force ratio is still decreasing, the fall of trend productivity is minor, the index of technical progress increases by 6.7 per cent and there is no further decline in OECD GDP.

The real price of oil and non-oil primaries, as well as the tax rates, show consistent changes, the first two fall by 62 per cent and 37 per cent respectively and the third one reduces its pace of growth from 4 to 0.1 p.p.. The slight improvement (or the pause in the deterioration) of most of the OECD economic indicators are associated, however, with a steady decline of the rate of growth of trend and actual GDP in LDC although its external debt, both in real terms and relative to trend GDP, grows at a lesser pace.

In order to examine the breakdown of the equilibrium values it is convenient to ideally group the exogenous determinants into homogeneous sets:

1. trending factors originated from the OECD (trend labour productivity, capital/labour force ratio, capital stock, technical progress, time trend);
2. trending factors originated from LDC (summarized by the trend LDC GDP and the coffee frost dummy);
3. OECD policy variables (taxes and OECD real government debt);
4. the real price of oil.

Results are reported in tables 4.3 to 4.10.

Table 4.3 Breakdown of the change of equilibrium OECD unemployment rate (percentage points)

	58–67 *to* *68–72*	*68–72* *to* *73–79*	*73–79* *to* *80–84*	*80–84* *to* *85–88*
OECD trend factors	–0.1774	0.5272	1.0298	0.6961
LDC trend factors & dummy	0.1469	0.1658	0.0303	0.0460
OECD policy factors:				
taxes	0.7191	0.6016	0.4841	0.0168
debt	0.1627	–0.0365	–0.0975	–0.0484
Real price of oil	–0.0759	0.3991	0.2723	–0.2218

Note: variable definition in the data appendix

4.7.2 Accounting for the change of equilibrium rate of unemployment

Although the relative significance of the exogenous determinants of the OECD unemployment rate changes considerably with time, two are the most important factors throughout the decades: the OECD tax policy and the real price of oil. Starting from the early 1970s the OECD trending factors have also an overall positive impact which is the combined effect of a positive influence due to the time trend and of a negative one due to the developments of labour productivity, capital stock and technical progress. However, between 1970s and early 1980s, the influence of these last factors reduces so that a considerable positive effect of OECD overall trending factors becomes clear. By that time the OECD tax policy and the real price of oil had somewhat reduced their effects in comparison with the previous period; in particular until the early 1970s the OECD fiscal policy played a considerable role on the rate of

unemployment but such an influence steadily declines thereafter. Finally, the impact of the price of oil, positive during the
two oil crises, becomes negative in the last period and accounts
for a 0.2 p.p. fall of the equilibrium unemployment rate.

4.7.3   Accounting for the change of equilibrium non-oil commodity price index

During the first sub-period the equilibrium real price of non-oil
primary commodities is affected by a few large negative
pressures originated by the rise of capital stock and technical
progress. Also the time trend carries, throughout, a negative
influence even if its strength declines from 11 per cent in the
first interval to 6.7 per cent in the last one.[12] Overall the impact
of the trending factors originating in the North is always
negative even though their importance is declining. Among the
trending factors originating in the South, trend LDC GDP
tends to raise the equilibrium price though its effect is rather
small and also declining through time from around 2.7 per cent
to 0.8 per cent. On the other hand, the dummy impact, evident
in the two central periods, produces a 6 per cent rise, and then
an equal fall.

The OECD fiscal policy generates a negative influence on
non-oil prices; this pressure is considerable in the second and
third interval, but modest in the first one, when the tax effect is
counterbalanced by a falling OECD debt / GDP ratio, and in
the last one, when the tax impact itself is much reduced. Finally
the importance of the oil price is particularly clear in the
intervals comprising the shocks when it shows up as the major
driving force.

4.7.4   Accounting for the change of equilibrium real wage

The development of the equilibrium real wage is largely
affected by the dramatic fall of the weight of trend labour
productivity: whereas labour productivity growth determines an
increase of the real wage equal to 19 per cent between 1958–67

Table 4.4 Breakdown of the change of equilibrium real non-oil primary
commodity price (percentage)

	58–67 to 68–72	68–72 to 73–79	73–79 to 80–84	80–84 to 85–88
OECD trend factors	−19.0600	−13.2126	−13.4040	−10.8640
LDC trend factors & dummy	2.7237	8.3019	−4.6666	0.8535
OECD policy factors:				
taxes	−3.8943	−3.2579	−2.6214	−0.0911
debt	3.0137	−0.6768	−1.8072	−0.8972
Real price of oil	−2.5307	13.3112	9.0835	−7.3977

Note: variable definition in the data appendix

and 1968–72, in the second interval this increase halves to 9 per cent and in the last two periods it reduces to 4 per cent. Overall the contribution of the OECD trending components determines an increase of the equilibrium real wage equal to 20 per cent in the first interval and to 6.5 per cent in the last one.

The increase in the tax rates determines a real wage growth which is around 2 per cent in each span of time except for the last one when the impact declines to less than 0.1 per cent.

On the other hand the real price of oil has a negligible effect on the equilibrium real wage and it is negative in two intervals: that is, once non-oil primaries, but particularly the real interest rate, are substituted out in the steady-state equation, real wages do not exhibit an effective resistance to oil price increases.

Finally one should point out the negative pressure generated by the ratio of OECD government debt to trend GDP the rise of which, particularly in the early 1980s, contributes to a 1.8 per cent fall in real wages.

Table 4.5   Breakdown of the change of equilibrium real wage
(percentage)

	58–67 to 68–72	68–72 to 73–79	73–79 to 80–84	80–84 to 85–88
OECD trend factors	20.5231	12.3189	8.4197	6.5056
LDC trend factors & dummy	2.7333	2.0670	1.5811	0.8565
OECD policy factors:				
taxes	2.5432	2.1276	1.7119	0.0595
debt	3.0242	–0.6791	–1.8135	–0.9004
Real price of oil	0.0531	–0.2795	–0.1907	0.1553

Note: variable definition in the data appendix

4.7.5   Accounting for the change of equilibrium real interest rate

Overall the OECD trending factors determine a positive change of the equilibrium real interest rate: in response to these forces the latter rises by 7 p.p. in the first intervals and by 2 p.p. in the last interval. Among the OECD trending factors the most important ones are the stock of capital, which induces a rise of the real interest rate and the capital/labour force ratio which causes a decline of the real interest rate. Once these North-originated trends are summed to the trending factors originated in the South the overall impact remains positive at the two extremes but is neutral in the central intervals. Then, in these periods, the development of the equilibrium real interest rate is determined by the unfolding of the oil price and by the OECD debt policy: both factors tend to raise the rate of interest. In the first interval falling debt and oil prices

Table 4.6 Breakdown of the change of equilibrium real interest rate
(percentage points)

	58–67 to 68–72	68–72 to 73–79	73–79 to 80–84	80–84 to 85–88
OECD trend factors	6.9894	3.3289	2.2231	2.1250
LDC trend factors & dummy	–3.8617	–2.6146	–2.5395	–1.2100
OECD policy factors:				
taxes	–0.3317	–0.2775	–0.2233	–0.0078
debt	–4.2725	0.9594	2.5621	1.2720
Real price of oil	–0.5165	2.7166	1.8538	–1.5097

Note: variable definition in the data appendix

compensate the positive trending pressure; in the final interval, however, debt policy is acting in the opposite direction and only the drastic fall of the real price of oil reduces the positive pressure from the trend factors.

4.7.6 Accounting for the change of equilibrium LDC real external debt

A large part of the rise of LDC external debt, especially in the first interval of time, is explained by trending factors originating in the North; their impact, although positive, declines at the beginning of the 1970s and then again in the subsequent years. In the first period the large positive pressure coming from the North is well counterbalanced by the growth of LDC trend GDP and by a falling OECD debt. However this last element, by reverting its rate of change from the early 1970s,

Table 4.7   Breakdown of the change of equilibrium real LDC external
debt (percentage)

	58–67 to 68–72	68–72 to 73–79	73–79 to 80–84	80–84 to 85–88
OECD trend factors	113.1153	53.8746	35.9786	34.3912
LDC trend factors & dummy	–20.7644	–9.5084	–18.2053	–6.5065
OECD policy factors:				
taxes	–5.3682	–4.4908	–3.6135	–0.1256
debt	–22.9739	5.1591	13.7768	6.8399
Real price of oil	–8.3586	43.9648	30.0014	–24.4335

Note: variable definition in the data appendix

eventually contributes to the rise of LDC debt via an upward
pressure on the real interest rate. Contemporaneously the oil
price shocks strike heavily on LDC debt while the decline in the
growth of LDC trend GDP hampers the potential compensat-
ing forces. The final decline of the oil price is the only factor
which effectively improves LDC external debt in the last
interval of time.

4.7.7   Accounting for the change of equilibrium LDC GDP

Given the specification used, equilibrium LDC GDP is
essentially determined by its trend. Positive deviations from it
appear to be linked, in the first interval, to the OECD trending
elements; however, in the following periods of time, the latter
are actually depressing LDC GDP, as does the OECD tax
policy. On the contrary, a rise of both OECD debt and oil
prices expands LDC GDP.

Table 4.8 Breakdown of the change of equilibrium real LDC GDP (percentage)

	58–67 to 68–72	68–72 to 73–79	73–79 to 80–84	80–84 to 85–88
OECD trend factors	0.5554	–0.0210	–0.3303	–0.1812
LDC trend factors & dummy	41.5743	32.5059	22.9823	13.0272
OECD policy factors:				
taxes	–0.3575	–0.2991	–0.2406	–0.0084
debt	–0.1719	0.0386	0.1031	0.0512
Real price of oil	–0.2270	1.1939	0.8147	–0.6635

Note: variable definition in the data appendix

4.8 THE SHORT-RUN: NOMINAL INERTIA AND THE DETERMINANTS OF WAGE AND PRICE FORECASTING ERRORS

Following the theoretical analysis presented in Chapter 2 it is interesting to use the estimated model to inquire into the determinants of wage and price forecasting errors. In order to accomplish this, the steady-state equations are augmented with short-run factors and wage and price forecasting errors so that the system considered is the following:[13]

$$p - w = -8.223 - 1.014(yt - l) - 3.268U + 0.583R$$
$$- 1.962(w - w^e)$$

$$w - p = 5.784 + 0.742(yt - l) + 0.226\chi(pc - p)$$
$$+ 1.777NC/N + 1.409U + 0.010t - 0.692R$$
$$- 0.516(p - p^e)$$

$$NC/N = 0.002 + 0.257T + 0.178\chi(pn - p) - 0.936U$$

$$pn - p = -0.519 - 0.179(s - p) + 0.270dum \tag{4.3}$$
$$- 6.751U + 0.214(po - p) - 7.000\Delta U$$
$$+ 0.327\Delta po + 7.219(il - is)$$

$$R = 1.019 + 0.062(s - p - yt^*) + 0.0463(e - p - yt)$$
$$- 1.976\Delta(m - p) + 3.304\Delta U + 2.626\Delta y$$

$$s - p = -15.582 + 0.715(pn - p) + 0.169(po - p)$$
$$+ 2.412y + 5.847R$$

In addition we estimate a simple relationship that links wage forecasting errors to price forecasting errors such that:

$$(w - w^e) = 0.5839(p - p^e) \tag{4.4}$$

By solving this system for price forecasting errors we obtain:

$$(p - p^e) = -2.207(U - U^*) - 0.393\Delta U + 0.257\Delta k$$
$$+ 0.123\Delta(k - l) - 0.230\Delta a + 0.0047\Delta po \tag{4.5}$$
$$+ 0.248\Delta(m - p) + 0.104(il - is)$$

where U^* is the long-run equilibrium rate of unemployment.

Table 4.9 reports the break-down of wage and price forecasting errors according to expression (4.5). It turns out

Table 4.9   Breakdown of wage and price forecasting errors (percentage)

	58–67 to 68–72	68–72 to 73–79	73–79 to 80–84	80–84 to 85–88
$U - U^*$	1.603	−1.356	−3.006	−0.524
ΔU	−0.092	−0.021	−0.184	0.430
Δk	0.174	−0.205	−0.264	−0.004
$\Delta(k - l)$	0.078	−0.138	−0.084	−0.038
Δa	0.384	0.389	−0.100	−0.269
Δpo	0.032	0.108	−0.058	−0.166
$(il - is)$	7.880	6.341	4.653	−8.277
$\Delta(m - p)$	−0.032	−0.619	−0.088	0.665

that the effect induced by the gap between U and U^* is always larger, in absolute value, than the effect caused by ΔU. In particular in the two central intervals both factors tend to depress inflation whereas in the two extreme periods they push in opposite directions: from 1958–67 to 1968–72 the rate of unemployment is rising but below its long-run; between 1980–84 and 1985–88 the rate of unemployment is falling but above its long-run value. However, in neither of these two cases is the effect of the change of the rate of unemployment sufficiently strong to dominate the imprint to inflation given by the long-run value. To investigate this question further we compute the change in inflation due to ΔU and $(U - U^*)$ for all those years in which these two components operate in opposite directions (that is $\Delta U > 0$ and $(U - U^*) < 0$ or vice-versa).[14] The only instance in which the impact of ΔU dominates that of $(U - U^*)$ is 1988 since at that date the change in U is sufficiently large (1 p.p.) whereas the distance from the long-run value is very small (0.08 p.p.).

In fact a comparison of the first two lines of Table 4.9 makes clear that the effect of ΔU on wage and price forecasting errors rises in importance throughout the years and becomes particularly relevant in the first half of the 1980s whereas the weight of the long-run component falls. The theoretical analysis suggests that such a situation, characterized by a rising importance of short-run factors, is likely to be associated with an increased persistence of the economic system.

4.9 HYSTERESIS OF THE OECD UNEMPLOYMENT RATE

In order to examine persistence and hysteresis we delimit the so-called short-run equilibrium by assuming that expectations are realized and letting the short-run *demand* factors extend into the long-run.[15] The short-run equilibrium so computed is characterized, in particular, by a short-run equilibrium NAIRU equal to 4.91 per cent hence lower than the long-run NAIRU. Indeed the short-run lines, though steeper than the long-run

Table 4.10 The persistence of U

| | Dependent Variable U_t^{S*} (Ordinary least squares) | | | |
	1958–88	1958–72	1973–88	1973–82
U_{t-1}	–0.034	–0.161	0.048	0.066
	(1.32)	(4.22)	(2.02)	(2.04)
U^*	1.020	1.449	0.916	0.902
	(28.69)	(11.58)	(33.84)	(27.84)
Δk	–0.064	–0.428	–0.014	–0.030
	(2.03)	(3.68)	(0.68)	(1.60)
$\Delta(k-l)$	–0.453	0.109	–0.245	0.107
	(1.60)	(0.35)	(0.64)	(0.25)
Δa	–0.066	–0.015	–0.110	–0.098
	(4.40)	(0.67)	(3.95)	(2.14)
se	0.00084	0.00074	0.00039	0.00032
R^2c	0.997	0.984	0.998	0.998
DW	1.24	1.30	2.93	2.78

ones, intersect at the left of the long-run lines.[16] This implies that, world-wide, hysteresis was not pervasive, in the sample period considered; indeed we know it to be a significant feature in only a few OECD countries.

Once the short-run equilibrium rate of unemployment (U^{S*}) has been etimated, we regress it on U^* and U_{-1}.[17] Results by sub-periods are reported in Table 4.10.

The estimated regressions confirm that the persistence of U increases after 1972; in fact, in the whole sample period (first column), the lagged component is insignificant and the short-run equilibrium rate of unemployment is closely linked to the long-term equilibrium one; positive deviations from it are induced by a declining growth of capital and technical progress. When the sample period is restricted to run from 1973 to 1988 (third column) the lagged rate of unemployment gains significance whereas the value of the coefficient on the long-term rate falls. Indeed the recursive estimates of the coefficient of lagged U increase until the early 1980s (see Figure 4.12)

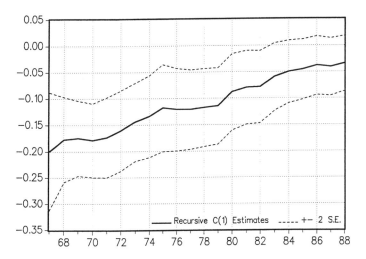

Figure 4.12   Recursive estimates of the coefficient of lagged U

whereas the recursive estimates of the coefficient of the long-run component, plotted in Figure 4.13, denote a declining trend which becomes particularly sharp from 1973 to 1976 and remains fairly stable thereafter.

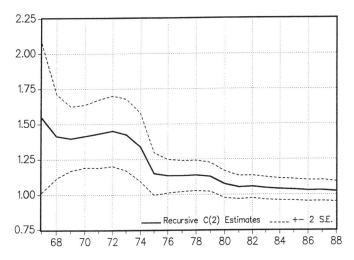

Figure 4.13   Recursive estimates of the coefficient of U^*

Table 4.11   The effect of the primary commodity market on the persistence of U: financial market exogenous

| | Dependent Variable Url_t^{S*} (Ordinary least squares) | | | |
	1958–88	*1958–72*	*1973–88*	*1973–82*
U_{t-1}	0.021	0.002	0.018	0.039
	(3.47)	(1.99)	(1.08)	(2.28)
Url^*	0.973	0.994	0.973	0.958
	(121.32)	(373.00)	(54.24)	(58.84)
Δk	0.015	0.005	0.022	0.005
	(2.10)	(1.93)	(1.62)	(0.49)
$\Delta(k-l)$	−0.066	−0.008	−0.202	0.222
	(0.97)	(1.24)	(0.74)	(0.95)
Δa	−0.002	−0.001	−0.011	−0.010
	(0.67)	(2.12)	(0.59)	(0.42)
se	0.00020	0.00002	0.00027	0.00017
R^2c	0.999	0.999	0.999	0.999
DW	2.17	2.16	2.71	2.99

The theoretical analysis developed in Chapter 2 showed that the endogenization of external markets could potentially revert the conclusions based on the restricted partial equilibrium case. In order to assess the role of external markets on the hysteresis property of the rate of unemployment, we perform a few regressions based on two restricted versions of the model: the first one (labelled $r1$ in Table 4.11) exogenizes the financial market, the second one (labelled $r2$ in Table 4.12) exogenizes the primary commodity market and LDC GDP.

The exclusion of financial market feedbacks makes the lagged rate of unemployment significant on the overall sample period and the value of its coefficient grows during the second half of the 1970s and then again at the end of the 1980s (figure 4.14). On the other hand recursive estimates of the long-run coefficient show a declining value particularly from the late 1970s and this is confirmed by sub-period regressions.

On the contrary, the exclusion of the primary commodity market and LDC goods market (Table 4.12) causes, on the

Table 4.12 The effect of the financial market on the persistence of U: primary commodity market exogenous

| | Dependent Variable $Ur2_t^{S*}$ (Ordinary least squares) | | | |
	1958–88	1958–72	1973–88	1973–82
U_{t-1}	0.012	0.051	–0.008	–0.017
	(1.46)	(3.78)	(1.22)	(1.91)
$Ur2^*$	0.985	0.814	1.011	1.019
	(88.76)	(20.39)	(156.98)	(118.03)
Δk	0.028	0.202	0.015	0.020
	(2.11)	(4.56)	(2.70)	(3.44)
$\Delta(k-l)$	0.189	–0.013	0.008	–0.150
	(1.56)	(0.11)	(0.07)	(1.19)
Δa	0.022	–0.008	0.032	0.036
	(3.08)	(0.84)	(3.16)	(2.58)
se	0.00036	0.00030	0.00010	0.00009
R^2c	0.999	0.998	0.999	0.999
DW	1.24	1.65	2.59	2.78

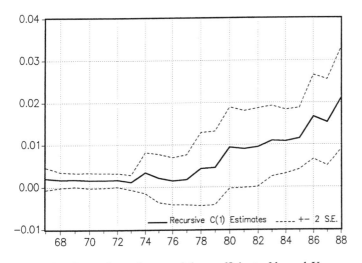

Figure 4.14 Recursive estimates of the coefficient of lagged U.
Restricted model: North + primary commodity + LDC GDP

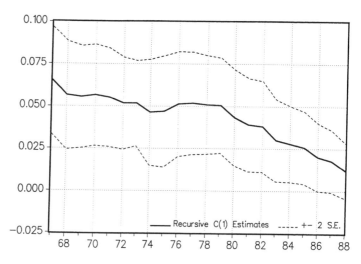

Figure 4.15 Recursive estimates of the coefficient of lagged U.
Restricted model: North + financial market

whole period, a decline in the significance of the lagged component. The latter also shows a decreasing coefficient (Figure 4.15) whereas that of the long-run component is rising.

In conclusion, feedbacks from the primary commodity market have increased the persistence of the rate of unemployment in the OECD, particularly from 1973 to 1982; the operation of the financial market appears to have acted, on the whole period and in the first sub-period in order to reduce the degree of persistence.

It is also clear that the effects of the interplay of OECD and external markets, are not simply the sum of the single impacts. This recommends us to study the role and the interaction of the different markets.

4.10   OIL SHOCK SIMULATIONS

The last empirical exercise simulates oil price shocks using the estimated model. We assume a permanent two-fold rise of the dollar price of oil and trig the shock ten years before the end of the sample so that a sufficient period of time is left for the shock to feed through.

In order to analyse the adjustment processes and the role of short-run factors, the simulation exercise is also performed on the long-run and on an augmented long-run model, as we shall call it, which includes short-run factors.[18] Moreover, to have some insight into the role of the various markets in transmitting the shock, the simulation is also performed on sub-sets of the model which alternatively exogenize some of the markets.

For each endogenous variable the base run is initially determined by dynamically simulating the model over the historical data; the base runs are confronted with the actual paths in Figures 4.4 to 4.11. The dynamic multiplier is then defined as the difference between the value of the variable in presence of the shock and the base run.[19]

4.10.1   The role of adjustment processes and short-run factors

The system, once hit by an exogenous oil price shock, and in absence of subsequent economic policy actions, does not automatically return to its previous equilibrium; on the assumption of a twofold rise of the nominal oil price, the new equilibrium is characterized by a higher rate of unemployment (+0.6 p.p.), higher real wages (+1.1 per cent), lower OECD GDP (–0.2 per cent), higher real interest rate (+1.5 p.p.), higher real LDC external debt (+24.6 per cent), higher real non-oil primary commodity prices (+6.3 per cent), higher LDC GDP (+0.6 per cent) and lower industrial conflicts per employee (–0.3 p.p.).

Figures 4.16 to 4.23 illustrate, for each endogenous variable, three multipliers obtained, separately, from the dynamic model, the long-run model and the augmented long-run model.

The working of the short-run demand factors alone, that is abstracted from the adjustment processes, does not appear to induce significantly different results from those ensued by the

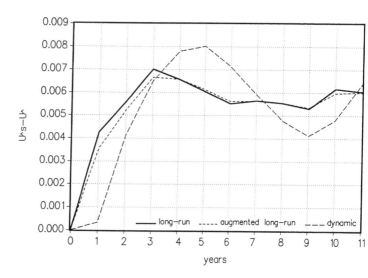

Figure 4.16   Rate of unemployment multipliers

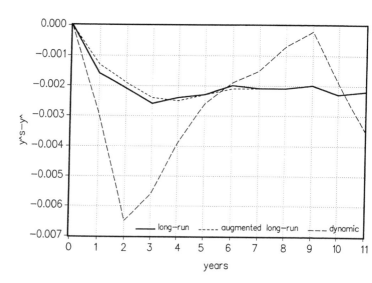

Figure 4.17   OECD GDP multipliers

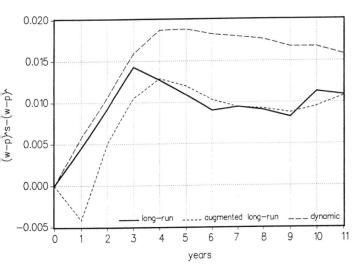

Figure 4.18   Real wage multipliers

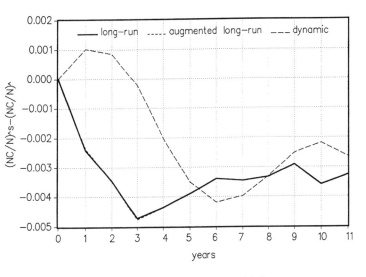

Figure 4.19   Normalized number of conflicts multipliers

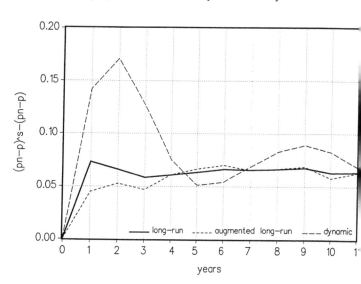

Figure 4.20   Real non-oil primary commodity price multipliers

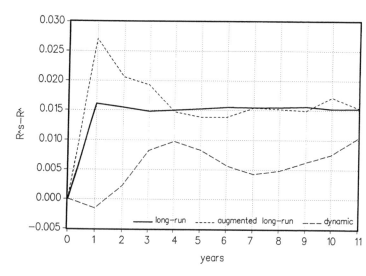

Figure 4.21   Real interest rate multipliers

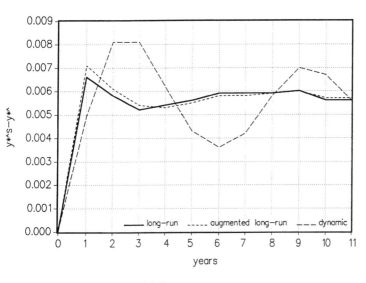

Figure 4.22 LDC GDP multipliers

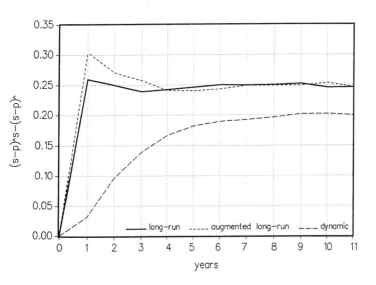

Figure 4.23 LDC real external debt multiplier

long-run model. Some divergences are evident, however, for the real interest rate which, in presence of short-run factors, temporarily overshoots its new long-run equilibrium by 1 p.p.; likewise the LDC real external debt rises above its long-run value by 5 per cent whereas real non-oil primary prices have an opposite reaction and temporarily fall below their new long-run value. In any case these deviations are short-lived and after three or four years the paths of the long-run and of the augmented long-run multipliers are close to each other.

The dynamic multipliers normally show a larger variability and the tendency to approach the long-run value by oscillating around the long-run multiplier. This happens to the rate of unemployment which hits an increase of 0.8 p.p. five years after the shock[20] and then declines, in the following four years, to 0.4 p.p., that is below the long-run increase of 0.6 p.p. OECD GDP initially falls below the long-run decrease and by the second year reaches –0.6 per cent; thereafter the multipliers rises and the ninth year after the shock it is close to zero and above the long-run multiplier which is around 0.2 per cent. Real non-oil primary commodity prices initially overshoot the long-run multiplier and rise by almost 17 per cent by the second year; afterwards they decline to the long-run and remains fairly stable around it (+6 per cent). LDC GDP initially overshoots its long-run multiplier (0.6 per cent) and by the second year it reaches +0.8 per cent ; thereafter it falls and oscillates around the long-run.

A different behaviour is shown by the dynamic multipliers of real wage, real interest rate and LDC external debt which do not exhibit an oscillating pattern around the long-run multiplier. The real wage increases by almost 2 per cent by the forth year and steadily declines thereafter to the lower long-run level (1 per cent). The adjustment process of the real interest rate wipes out the overshooting due to short-run demand factors and the long-run value is slowly reached by increasing towards it. A similar development is shown by the LDC real external debt: the overshooting disappears and the long-run multipliers are reached gradually from below.

4.10.2 The role of single external markets on the OECD economy

In order to discern the role of the different markets in propagating the shock, we start from an initial restricted version of the model which includes the Northern markets only; this sub-system in then extended by adding the remaining non-OECD markets. Notice that each restricted version is derived by re-estimating the model using the corresponding sub-system of equations and not simply by excluding some equations from the original estimated complete model. Hence the discrepancy between the corresponding multipliers is not only explained by the exogenization or otherwise of a particular equation but also reflects the fact that such exogenization modifies the coefficient set of each estimated restricted model.

The impact of external markets on the OECD variables (rate of unemployment, GDP, real wage, inflation and number of conflicts) is initially discussed by comparing, for each variable, the overall multiplier with those obtained by adding the external markets one at a time. That is the North-restricted version of the model, call it NORTH, is augmented by the LDC GDP equation to obtain a less restricted model, call it R1; then the same North-restricted model is augmented with the non-oil primary commodity equation to obtain the restricted model R2; analogously, model R3 is obtained by adding the LDC debt equation to the initial NORTH model and model R4 is obtained by adding the real interest rate equation. Figure 4.24 outlines the sub-sets.

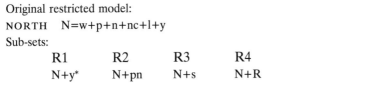

Original restricted model:
NORTH   N=w+p+n+nc+l+y
Sub-sets:

R1	R2	R3	R4
N+y*	N+pn	N+s	N+R

Figure 4.24   The restricted models

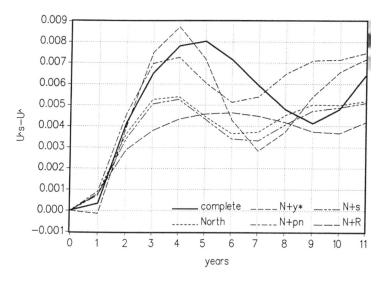

Figure 4.25   Rate of unemployment dynamic multipliers

If all non-OECD markets are exogenous, that is if we use the North-restricted model, the response of the OECD rate of unemployment to an oil price shock is less pronounced than in the complete case and increases, at the maximum, by 0.5 p.p. (Figure 4.25). In fact the path followed by this restricted multiplier remains quite similar to the original multiplier: most of the increase is within the first four years and thereafter the rate of unemployment declines to the lower long-run level. The endogenization of LDC GDP and non-oil primary commodity prices sharpens the increase of the rate of unemployment and LDC GDP, in particular, magnifies the variability of the response as well. On the other hand, the endogenization of the financial market reduces the increase of the rate of unemployment: in particular the real interest rate, when allowed to feedback, determines both a reduction of the oil shock impact on the rate of unemployment as well as an elongation and a levelling of the cyclicality of the response of the rate of unemployment; this confirms the so-called

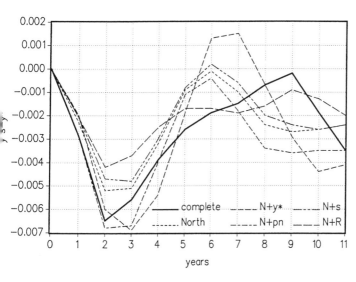

Figure 4.26 OECD GDP dynamic multipliers

'absorbtion' result which we detected from the graphical analysis of the long-run solution.

Likewise, the North-restricted OECD GDP multiplier shows, relative to the overall model multiplier, both a less pronounced initial decline and a faster successive improvement (Figure 4.26); moreover the inactivity of external feedbacks reduces the length of the cycle induced by the shock. When the feedbacks from LDC GDP and non-oil primary commodity prices are allowed to operate, the fall in the first three years deepens, as happens for the rate of unemployment. Likewise, the feedbacks from LDC GDP widen the variability of the OECD GDP response and intensify the oscillating pattern. A contrary force originates from the financial market and in particular from the real interest rate which attenuates the initial decline as well as the successive fluctuations while it lengthens the cyclical pattern.

The dynamic response of OECD inflation to an oil price increase (Figure 4.27) is minimum when no external markets

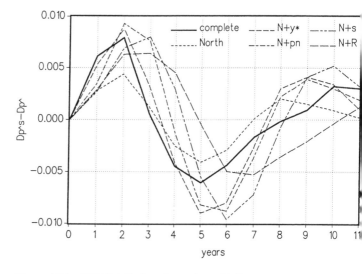

Figure 4.27   OECD inflation dynamic multipliers

are endogenized; when feedbacks are taken into account th
initial upsurge in inflation increases and the variability i
normally sharper. However, it should be noticed that inflatio
starts declining two years after the shock and this is true even i
restricted NORTH model, that is even in absence of feedback
from external markets.

On the other hand, the positive role played by the financia
market is again clear for the real wage (Figure 4.28). The
North-restricted multiplier, which is below the overall one, get
further reduced by the operation of both the real interest rat
and the LDC external debt. On the other hand LDC GDP and
above all, non-oil primary commodity prices, increase the ris
of the real wage in response to an oil shock.

According to the North-restricted model industrial conflict
undergo a declining trend in response to an oil price shoc
(Figure 4.29); however, if the feedbacks from the externa
markets are taken into account, the fall is evident only from th
third year: before that strikes show a moderate rise. This initia
upsurge of industrial action is basically linked to th

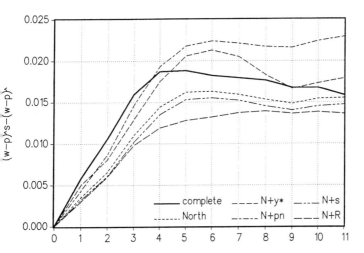

Figure 4.28 Real wage dynamic multipliers

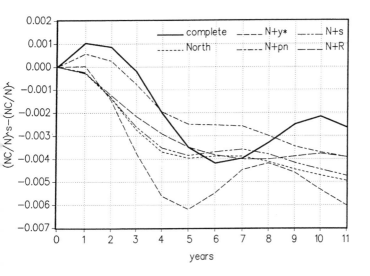

Figure 4.29 Normalized number of conflict dynamic multipliers

endogenization of non-oil commodity prices: the rise which the latter undergo following the oil shock, provides a relevant direct impulse to conflicts even in presence of a higher rate of unemployment which activates a counterbalancing force. On the other hand, the endogenization of LDC GDP, since it impresses its effects only via the rate of unemployment, causes a further fall of industrial strife. The financial market has only a moderate impact though the real interest rate, again, evens out the variability of the multiplier.

4.10.3   The propagation of the oil shock to the whole system

In a second exercise the external markets are added sequentially to the initial North-restricted model so to recover at the end of the procedure, the overall system of equations. At each stage the dynamic multipliers of the endogenous variables are computed so that the final multipliers results from a progression of multipliers which gradually endogenize an increasing number of equations. For the non-OECD variables the initial restricted model is the NORTH plus their own equation.[21]

As far the OECD economy is concerned, the sequential inclusion of the external markets basically confirms the points highlighted in the previous exercise. The rise of the rate of unemployment, which reaches 0.5 p.p. in the forth year according to the North-restricted model, rises to almost 0.8 p.p. by including LDC GDP and slightly more by further adding the primary commodity market; however, whereas the rise induced by pn is partially persistent, that ascribable to y^* is short-lasted. Finally the inclusion of the financial market makes U decline to 0.75 p.p. (Figure 4.30).

By the fifth year the rise of the real wage is just above 1.5 per cent according to the North-restricted model; it rises to over 2 per cent by adding LDC GDP and to 2.5 per cent by further adding non-oil primary prices; then it declines again to around 2 per cent by summing the effects of the real interest rate (Figure 4.32).

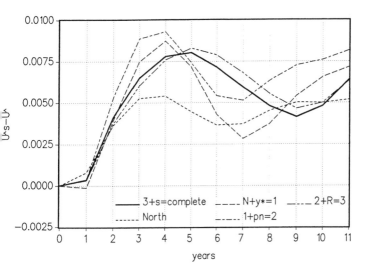

Figure 4.30   Rate of unemployment sequential multipliers

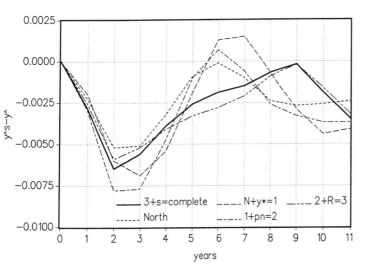

Figure 4.31   OECD GDP sequential multipliers

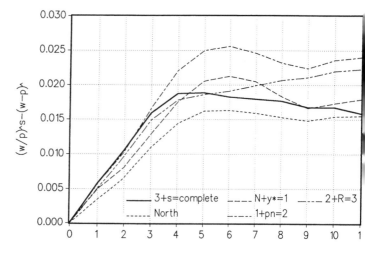

Figure 4.32   Real wage sequential multipliers

According to the North-restricted model industrial conflicts start declining from the first year after the shock; the inclusion of LDC GDP defers the start of the decline to the second year but impresses a more pronounced fall thereafter. The successive inclusion of non-oil primary commodity prices and of the real interest rate induce a moderate rise of the conflicts in the first two years and determine a less pronounced decline throughout the following period (Figure 4.33).

Two years after the shock inflation in the OECD has risen by almost 1 per cent (Figure 4.34); this is the maximum increase and by the end of the sample, inflation is back to its initial level. Feedbacks from global markets tend to rise the inflationary impact of the oil shock: if all external markets are excluded the rise is, at most 0.5 per cent. In particular feedbacks from LDC demand increase the average impact as well as its variability; likewise the response from the non-oil primary market tends to rise inflation although by a smaller amount; on the contrary the operation of the financial market shows a moderate negative pressure on inflation.

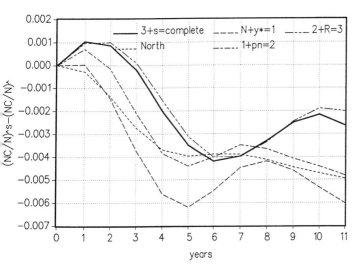

Figure 4.33   Normalized number of conflict sequential multipliers

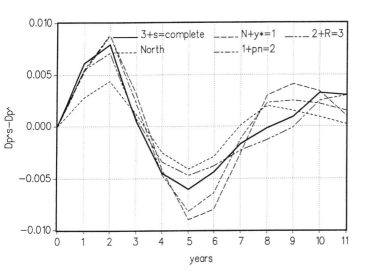

Figure 4.34   OECD inflation sequential multipliers

The price of non-oil primary commodities rises, in real terms, by around 17 per cent by the second year after the shock; thereafter it falls sharply to its long-run multiplier as U rises (Figure 4.35). The initial restricted multiplier, obtained from a model which adds the primary commodity market to the North-restricted system, shows, relative to the complete one, a lesser tendency to decline to the long-run value so that the rise of non-oil prices remains around 10 per cent instead of falling towards 5 per cent. The major non-OECD force depressing the real price of non-oil primaries after the shock is the level of LDC external debt; a minor role is left to the real interest rate and to LDC demand.

In shaping the response of the real interest rate to the oil price shock non-OECD pressures appear to be quantitatively more important than OECD ones (Figure 4.36). Particularly influential are the feedbacks from LDC GDP which nearly double the rise of the real interest rate due to the Northern pressures: according to the initial restricted model the real interest rate rises, by the fourth year, by 0.25 p.p.; this rises to

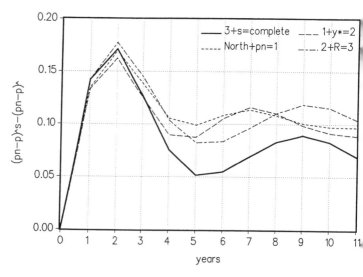

Figure 4.35 Non-oil primary commodity price sequential multipliers

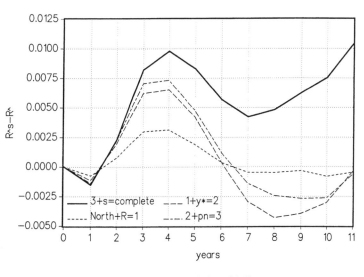

Figure 4.36   Real interest rate sequential multipliers

0.65 p.p. by further adding LDC GDP, to 0.75 p.p. by including the non-oil primary commodity price feedback and finally to 1 p.p. by adding the LDC external debt response. Notice however that, as expected from the equation specification, non-oil primary commodity prices impress only a temporary impact whereas the endogenization of the LDC real external debt induces an upward trend on the multiplier.

The oil price shock raises LDC GDP; however the increase is, at most, 0.75 per cent suggesting that the shock-induced OECD recession, together with the rise of pn, though not sufficient to reverse the direction of the change, are exerting a downward pressure (Figure 4.37). If the feedbacks from the financial market and from the non-oil primary commodity market are excluded, the initial rise of LDC GDP, which shows up within the first three years, exceeds 1 per cent; the inclusion of the real interest rate slightly increases this effect. On the contrary the endogenization of non-oil primary commodity prices generates a conspicuous fall of LDC GDP whose growth, by the second year, falls to 0.7 per cent.

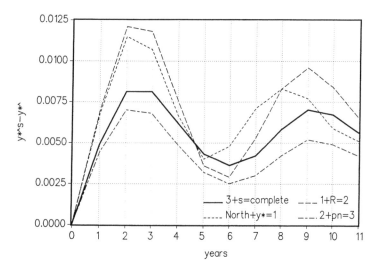

Figure 4.37   LDC GDP sequential multipliers

The operation of the North economy alone determines, by the sixth year after the shock, a 10 per cent rise of LDC real external debt (Figure 4.38). An additional important pressure which counts for almost another 5 per cent increase is the surge of non-oil prices and, even more important is the real interest rate which takes the rise of LDC external debt to 20 per cent in real terms; a minor role is ascribable to LDC GDP.

4.10.4   A summary of the oil shock effects

We may summarize the main results concerning the role played by the different markets in transmitting an oil price shock in the following points:

1. The feed-backs originating from the LDC aggregate demand increase both the average value and the variability of the rate of unemployment and OECD GDP. A significant positive pressure also comes from the feedback of non-oil primary commodity prices whereas the working of the

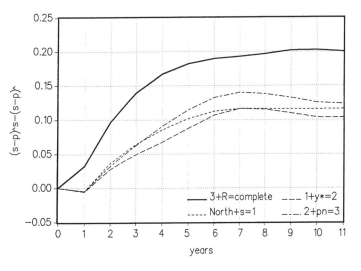

Figure 4.38 LDC real external debt sequential multiplier

financial market tends to absorb part of the raise of U and, most of all, absorbs some of its shock-induced variance.

2. The real wage resistance is enhanced by the additional increase of non-oil prices and dampened by financial market effects.

3. External market doubles the inflationary pressure successive to an oil price shock. If all external markets are excluded inflation rises, at most by 0.5 per cent, otherwise it increases by as much as 1 per cent. However, inflation falls after two years and the decline would come about even in absence of external markets.

4. As the recession induced in the North by the oil shock propagates through the system, the real price of non-oil primaries, which undergoes an immediate surge of 17 per cent, starts declining. This depressing tendency is enhanced by the rising level of LDC external debt; a minor role is left to the real interest rate and to LDC demand.

5. The real interest rate, though not directly affected by the oil shock, receives influential and lasting positive effect from

the rise of the LDC real external debt. Feedbacks from LDC GDP and from non-oil primary commodity prices also exert a positive though only temporary impact.

6. The response of the real interest rate to the oil shock raises LDC external debt by more than 5 per cent on top of the 10 per cent rise attributable to the North recession; a further positive effect comes from non-oil prices whereas only a minor role is played by LDC aggregate demand.

7. LDC aggregate demand is directly and positively affected by the oil price shock; this effect is counterbalanced by the North recession and by the rise of non-oil prices; these opposite effects then determine an overall negligible impact of the shock on the whole region.

From these results a few important considerations emerge.

The North bears the negative effects of an oil shock in terms of increased unemployment, depressed demand and higher inflation. On the whole the feedbacks from the global markets tend to exacerbate these costs though it is clear that, whereas the functioning of the financial market absorbs some of these losses, both in terms of magnitude and volatility, the primary commodity market and LDC aggregate demand tend to aggravate them.

The response of the real interest rate is to a great extent induced by the rise of LDC external debt that is, the beneficial 'shock absorbtion' in the North is at the expense of higher external debt and sharper GDP fluctuations in the South.

In the OECD there appears to be an internal tendency to adjust, at least partially, to the stock. In particular, even by excluding the eventual decline of *pn* due to rising OECD unemployment, OECD inflation finally declines.

APPENDIX TO CHAPTER 4: THE ESTIMATED MODEL
1958–1988 3SLS

OECD Product Market

Production function: Dependent variable $y_t - k_t$

c	−4.567	(3.34)
$y_{t-1} - k_{t-1}$	0.468	(4.95)
$y_{t-2} - k_{t-2}$	−0.090	(1.11)
k_t	−0.137	(1.61)
$n_t - k_t$	1.148	(7.86)
$n_{t-1} - k_{t-1}$	−0.916	(5.81)
a_t	0.433	(8.46)
se	0.00733	
R^2c	0.999	
DW	1.917	
LM	0.577	
$F(7, 17)$	0.87	

Steady-state solution

$$y - k = -7.335 + 0.372(n - k) - 0.220k + 0.696a$$

Price equation: Dependent variable $p_t - w_t$

c	−2.156	(6.23)
$p_{t-1} - w_{t-1}$	1.449	(14.78)
$p_{t-2} - w_{t-2}$	−0.712	(9.09)
$yt_{t-1} - l_{t-1}$	−0.266	(6.24)
R_t	−0.298	(4.49)
R_{t-1}	0.451	(7.78)
$(U_t + U_{t-1})/2$	−0.857	(5.12)
wfe_t	−0.514	(9.37)
se	0.00385	
R^2c	0.999	
DW	2.12	
LM	−0.918	
$F(8, 15)$	0.35	

Steady-state solution

$$p - w = -8.223 - 1.014(yt - l) - 3.268U + 0.583R$$

OECD labour market

Wage equation: Dependent variable $w_t - p_t$

c	1.876	(4.03)
$w_{t-1} - p_{t-1}$	0.676	(12.41)
$yt_t - l_t$	0.241	(4.43)
$\chi(pc_t - p_t)$	0.073	(2.14)
NC_t/N_t	0.577	(4.69)
R_{t-1}	-0.224	(2.08)
U_{t-1}	0.457	(2.14)
t	0.003	(1.76)
pfe_{t-1}	-0.167	(1.67)
se	0.00567	
R^2c	0.999	
DW	1.70	
LM	0.170	
$F(9, 13)$	0.98	

Steady-state solution

$$w - p = 5.784 + 0.742(yt - l) + 0.226\chi(pc - p) + 1.777NC/N$$
$$+ 1.409U + 0.010t - 0.629R$$

Number of conflict equation: dependent variable NC_t

$N_t c$	0.062	(0.07)
$N_t NC_{t-1}$	0.629	(6.27)
$N_t T_t$	0.095	(2.41)
$N_t \chi(pn_t - p_t)$	0.066	(1.78)
$N_t U_t$	-0.347	(3.25)
se	1611.0 (mean of $NC_t = 13397$)	
R^2c	0.848	
DW	1.85	
LM	-0.101	
$F(5, 21)$	0.11	

Steady-state solution

$$NC/N = 0.002 + 0.257T + 0.178\chi(pn - p) - 0.936U$$

Labour Force Equation: Dependent Variable l_t

c	12.312	(4250.8)
Δl_{t-1}	0.420	(4.40)
$\Delta(w_t - p_t)$	–0.296	(5.91)
pfe_t	–0.083	(1.76)
t	0.012	(140.00)
se	0.00407	
R^2c	0.999	
DW	1.69	
LM	0.268	
$F(5, 21)$	0.08	

Steady-state solution

$$l = 12.312 + 0.012t$$

OECD aggregate demand

OECD aggregate demand equation: Dependent variable y_t

c	1.053	(4.30)
y_{t-1}	1.003	(7.66)
y_{t-2}	–0.231	(1.83)
$m_t - p_t$	0.195	(4.24)
Δy_t^*	0.337	(3.08)
Δp_t	–0.142	(1.75)
$\Delta^2 p_t$	–0.420	(2.86)
se	0.00848	
R^2c	0.999	
DW	2.29	
LM	–0.125	
$F(7, 17)$	0.13	

Steady-state solution

$$y = 4.615 + 0.855(m - p)$$

LDC aggregate demand

LDC aggregate demand: Dependent variable $y_t^* - yt_t^*$

c	0.035	(3.11)
$y_{t-1}^* - yt_{t-1}^*$	0.856	(8.78)
$y_{t-2}^* - yt_{t-2}^*$	−0.651	(6.83)
$\Delta(y_t - yt_t)$	0.352	(3.94)
U_{t-1}	−0.496	(3.02)
$pn_t - p_t$	−0.019	(1.94)
$po_t - p_t$	0.012	(3.16)
se	0.00680	
$R^2 c$	0.999	
DW	2.11	
LM	−1.236	
$F(7, 17)$	0.25	

Steady-state solution

$$y^* = yt^* + 0.044 - 0.624U - 0.023(pn - p) + 0.016(po - p)$$

Primary commodity market

Non-oil primary price equation: Dependent variable Δpn_t

c	−0.343	(1.35)
Δpn_{t-1}	0.381	(3.48)
Δpo_t	0.216	(5.36)
ΔU_t	−4.616	(1.63)
$il - is_{t-1}$	4.761	(2.70)
$pn_{t-1} - p_{t-1}$	−0.659	(5.17)
$s_{t-1} - p_{t-1}$	−0.118	(3.95)
$po_{t-1} - p_{t-1}$	0.141	(2.60)
U_{t-1}	−4.453	(2.15)
dum	0.178	(3.94)

se	0.06298	
R^2c	0.981	
DW	1.81	
LM	0.35	
$F(10, 11)$	0.40	

Steady-state solution

$$pn - p = -0.519 - 0.179(s - p) + 0.270dum - 6.751U$$
$$+ 0.214(po - p)$$

Financial market

Real interest rate equation: Dependent variable R_t

c	0.240	(3.03)
R_{t-1}	0.764	(8.95)
$s_{t-2} - p_{t-2} - yt^*_{t-2}$	0.0146	(3.37)
$e_{t-1} - p_{t-1} - yt_{t-1}$	0.0109	(2.10)
ΔU_t	0.779	(1.94)
$\Delta(m - p)_{t-1}$	-0.466	(6.64)
Δy_t	0.619	(4.97)
se	0.00760	
R^2c	0.896	
DW	2.54	
LM	-1.569	
$F(7, 17)$	0.251	

Steady-state solution

$$R = 1.019 + 0.062(s - p - yt^*) + 0.046(e - p - yt)$$

LDC external debt equation: Dependent variable $s_t - p_t$

c	-5.893	(4.05)
$s_{t-1} - p_{t-1}$	0.622	(7.01)
$pn_t - p_t$	0.270	(3.64)
$po_{t-1} - p_{t-1}$	0.064	(2.47)
y_t	2.108	(2.79)
y_{t-1}	-1.196	(1.68)
R_{t-1}	2.211	(3.51)

se	0.06616
R^2c	0.998
DW	2.01
LM	0.052
$F(7, 17)$	0.212

Steady-state solution

$$s - p = -15.582 + 5.847R + 0.715(pn - p) + 0.169(po - p) + 2.412y$$

Notes to the tables

- t statistics in parenthesis.

- The LM test is a modified Lagrange Multiplier to test for a first order autocorrelation in the presence of lagged dependent variable and instrumental variables. The test is performed by running two stages least squares and then regressing the dependent variable on the original explanatory variables plus the first lag of the residuals obtained from the initial regression; the set of instruments used is the same in the two regressions. See Godfrey (1978) and Breusch (1978).

- The Chow Test on parameters stability is computed with split at 1972 as follows:

$$\frac{[\text{TRSS} - (\text{RSS1} + \text{RSS2})]/k}{(\text{RSS1} + \text{RSS2})/(\text{obs} - 2k)},$$

k being the number of explanatory variables plus the constant, TRSS, RSS1 and RSS2 indicating total and restricted sum of squared residuals; the test is distributed as $F(k, obs - 2k)$.

- The instruments used in the 3SLS procedure are: constant, dummies, trend, a, R_{t-2}, y_{t-1}, yt_t, k, k_{t-1}, pfe_t, T_{t-1}, T_{t-2}, m_{t-1}, m_{t-2}, U_{t-1}, $(g-p)_{t-1}$, n_{t-1}, n_{t-2}, $(p-w)_{t-1}$, $(p-w)_{t-2}$, inv_{t-1}, inv_{t-2}, y^*_{t-1}, $(pn-p)_{t-1}$, $(pn-p)_{t-2}$, $(s-p)_{t-1}$, $(e-p)_{t-1}$, h_{t-1}, NC/N_{t-1}.

5 Conclusions

We started this research with one major objective in mind: to understand how primary commodity prices affect the economic performance of the OECD; in fact, the basic consideration that the OECD countries spawn most of the demand for primaries, substantiated the idea that the causal relationship between commodity prices and the OECD economy runs both ways and that an explanation, to be exhaustive, must explicitly account for this fact.

In these concluding notes we briefly recollect the phases of this research and summarize the main results.

5.1 THE DESCRIPTIVE ANALYSIS

We began with some preliminary statistical information.

1. Between 1950 and 1992, the standard deviations of the detrended price series of oil, non-oil and of the OECD GDP deflator are respectively 0.61, 0.42 and 0.12.

   The sharper volatility of primary commodity prices relative to manufactured goods prices, though not a novelty, is a key starting point of our analysis: a fundamental assumption of the theoretical model is that the price determination mechanisms of oil, non-oil and manufactured-goods differ substantially: in particular, the characteristics of primary commodities make their prices quite responsive to demand-and-supply imbalances whereas manufactured goods prices are mostly driven by cost considerations.

2. The weight of primary commodities in the world trade structure is geographically uneven. In the early 1960s the percentage of primary commodities on total export revenues was nearly 90 per cent for the developing countries

150

and only 30 per cent for the OECD; by the late 1980s these shares have fallen respectively to 50 per cent and 20 per cent while at the same time the percentage of manufactured goods has risen from 64 per cent to 78 per cent in the OECD and from 11 per cent to 48 per cent in the LDC.

3. In addition many LDC economies suffer from an insufficient diversification in production: in the mid 1970s the IMF counted that 87 LDC economies depended on a few primaries and that a single commodity generated as much as 30 per cent of exports in 75 per cent of these countries. Still in 1992 (World Bank) 29 per cent of the low- and middle-income economy exports were made up by fuels, minerals and metals and 18 per cent by other primary commodities. This unbalanced economic structure makes it difficult for most of the LDC economies to hedge against primary price volatility and this may easily feed-back to the North's economy. Moreover, industrialized countries are heavily dependent on primary commodity imports: in the early 1990s they absorbed 80 per cent of their own primary commodity production and 70 per cent of that exported by LDC.

4. Fuels accounts for a significant proportion of LDC primary commodity exports: only 27 per cent of the world fuel exports originates from the OECD whereas the LDC's share is 49 per cent (data refer to the end of the 1980s). The percentage of fuels on OECD imports rose from 22 per cent in 1963 to 30.6 per cent in 1973 and to 57.6 per cent in 1980; thereafter it fell and reached 53.8 per cent in 1984 and to 38.7 per cent in 1987. More specifically, the share of oil in the world primary energy consumption increased from 31 per cent in 1960 to almost 50 per cent in 1973 and then fell to around 40 per cent. The increased importance of oil, coupled with the extraordinary fluctuations of its price, which were mainly dictated by events exogenous to economics, induced deep and abrupt transformations in the world economy.

5. Partly as a consequence of the enormous re-distribution of the world wealth and political power spurred by the oil

shocks, the 1970s witnessed a rapid growth in capital flows mainly directed to LDC economies; this tied further industrial and developing countries. The importance of the capital market emerged forcefully in conjunction with the debt crisis of the early 1980s and it now appears to be a powerful and quick-responding link between the world economies.

5.2   THE VECTOR AUTOREGRESSION ANALYSIS

As an initial statistical substantiation of the relationships emerging from the facts we performed Granger causality and cointegration tests on a simple VAR.

The Granger causality tests confirm that real primary commodity prices Granger-cause the OECD rate of unemployment, given the real interest rate; however the reverse causality is evident only if nominal primary commodity prices are used, that is, the OECD rate of unemployment Granger-causes nominal primary commodity prices, given the nominal short-term interest rate. Moreover the short-term nominal interest rate is important in forecasting nominal primary commodity prices, given the OECD rate of unemployment but nominal commodity prices do not Granger-cause the short-term nominal interest rate.

Cointegration analysis supports the existence of a two-way long-run relationship between OECD economic activity and primary commodity prices as long as both oil and non-oil prices are present. When the two price components are distinguished and simultaneously enter the VAR, a third significant relationship appears which seems to substantiate the endogeneity of the financial market and its long-run linkages with OECD economic activity and the primary commodity market.

5.3   THE BASIC FEATURES OF THE MODEL

We then proceeded to define the macroeconomic model. The strategy was to adopt a bloc model according to which OECD and LDC are taken as single regions bridged by several links, the most important being the primary commodity- and the financial market. This framework meets two basic requirments: first of all it allows the explicit simultaneous account for both the economic activity of the industrialized countries and the formation of commodity prices. Second, it is empirically functional and permits a clear understanding of the interactions between the variables of interest.

The theoretical model takes the moves from the working of the OECD economy described within an imperfectly competitive paradigm based on the labour market of the type Layard and Nickell (1986) have made standard. This framework is significantly extended by endogenizing the primary commodity market, LDC aggregate demand and the financial market which in turn comprises the real interest rate equation and the LDC external debt equation. The basic Layard-Nickell structure is also augmented, within the OECD economy, by the explicit account for industrial conflicts, aggregate demand and production function.

The long-run solution of the model is graphically illustrated in the $U - (pn - p)$ space by two lines: the North line representing the equilibrium in the OECD economy, and the South line, representing equilibrium in the South. Their empirical counterparts show that the locus of points of equilibrium for the North associates rising primary commodity prices to rising rates of unemployment; on the other hand the South's line is downward sloping and associates rising rates of U to declining primary commodity prices. Their intersection determines the average long-run rate of unemployment at 5.45 per cent.

5.4 EXTERNAL MARKETS AND HYSTERESIS OF THE OECD UNEMPLOYMENT RATE

In the short-run the system is normally away from the equilibrium thereby entailing changing inflation and price forecasting errors. The extent to which the system tends to persist away from the equilibrium is also a relevant feature and has attracted growing attention specially since the rate of unemployment was thought to exhibit some hysteresis. Indeed if the rate of unemployment includes a rising trend, as currently seems to be the case, hysteresis means mounting difficulties in reverting the direction of change and returning to previous values.

Using the theoretical model we show how the working of the primary commodity market and the financial market may affect hysteresis in the rate of unemployment. By applying this approach to the estimated model, we find that the persistence of the rate of unemployment increased from 1973 onwards and that the feedbacks from the primary commodity market played a primal role in this process whereas the operation of financial market pushed in the opposite direction therby inhibiting the forces of hysteresis. However, since hysteresis is highest when both markets are included, their interactions are likely to exert further pressure on persistence.

Although some persistence is clear, the evidence reveal that, in the period considered, a typical hysteresis situation was not prevailing in the OECD as a whole. This is confirmed by the fact that the so-called short-run NAIRU is, on average, a little lower than the long-run, conventional NAIRU. This also implies that short-run demand factors are not sufficiently strong to steer inflation in the direction contrary to the one indicated by the long-run equilibrium anchor.

5.5   WHAT HAVE WE LEARNED ABOUT THE LINKS BETWEEN PRIMARY COMMODITY PRICES AND THE OECD ECONOMIC PERFORMANCE?

The theoretical model, estimated on historical data, proved to be a useful device to appraise the relationships between the rate of unemployment and commodity prices, and more generally, the links between U and the various markets we explicitated.

A first information is obtained from the estimated coefficients of each single equation. Evidence on the equilibrium paths of the endogenous variables is obtained from the reduced form of the steady-state system. The more specific objective of understanding how the propagation mechanism works, that is, in particular, how the links operate and interact in the aftermath of an oil price shock, is attained by performing oil price simulations and computing the corresponding dynamic multipliers.

5.5.1 Through which channels do commodity prices feed into the North?

There are three possible *immediate* channels to convey primary price fluctuations to the Northern economy. One of these is through wage resistance, both in the wage and in the conflict equation, the second one is through aggregate demand and the third one may operate via the price mark-up.

The empirical evidence gave credit to the first one; in particular real wages appear to respond to a total primary commodity price index but a further effect on the non-oil component is introduced via the conflicts wave activated because of union's wage resistance: overall the long-run real wage elasticity to non-oil primary commodity prices is 0.036.

There are, of course, important *second-order* links, namely those originated in non-OECD markets and then fed to the North. These work via LDC demand, which is an explanatory variable of OECD GDP, and via the real interest rate which affects price and wage determination.

5.5.2 Through which channels does the North economy affect external markets?

There is only one *immediate* impact of the OECD economy on commodity prices and this is via the effect exerted by the rate of unemployment on non-oil primary prices: a 1 p.p. increase of the rate of unemployment determines a short-run fall of the nominal commodity price equal to 4.6 per cent and a fall of the real price equal, in the long-run, to 6.7 per cent.

There is, however, a major *second-order* link due to the presence, in the non-oil price equation, of the LDC external debt which captures the tendency of highly indebted non-oil exporting LDC to spur their exports by depreciating their currency and/or increasing commodity supply.

As long as a rise of the rate of unemployment rises the real interest rate, the LDC external debt increases and thereby aggravates the declining process of non-oil primaries. On the other hand, as a GDP decline in the North tends to lower the LDC external debt, the propensity to devalue or to boost supply and hence the fall of non-oil primary prices is, at least partially, offset.

Finally the OECD business cycle is the most important factor in determining deviations of LDC GDP from trend.

5.5.3   What is the role of the financial market?

The financial market operates by intersecting the information seized by the overall economic system and then feeding it back again to the various markets. The real interest rate is directly affected by OECD monetary and fiscal policies, through the growth of real money supply, the level of government debt and indicators of the business cycle, and it is also responsive to the LDC external debt.

The real interest rate is a significant explanatory variable in the price and wage equations as well as in the LDC external debt function. The impact of commodity prices on the financial market operates via the LDC debt equation. Both components of primary prices worsen LDC external debt; however a rise in the price of non-oil primaries produces a larger effect than the rise of oil, the two long-run elasticities being respectively 0.71 and 0.17.

5.6   HOW DOES THE SYSTEM REACT TO EXOGENOUS PRIMARY COMMODITY PRICE SHOCKS?

A hypothetical permanent two-fold increase of the dollar price of oil produces, in the long-run, a new equilibrium which, relative to the initial one, is characterized by a higher rate of unemployment (+0.6 p.p.), higher real wages (+1.1 per cent), lower OECD GDP (–0.2 per cent), higher real interest rate (+1.5 p.p.), higher real LDC external debt (+24.6 per cent), higher real non-oil primary commodity prices (+6.3 per cent), higher LDC GDP (+0.6 per cent) and lower industrial conflicts per employee (–0.3 p.p.).

The analysis of the role played by the various markets in propagating the shock shows that the Northern economy, on the whole, does not benefit from the feedbacks coming from external markets: rate of unemployment, inflation, aggregate demand and real wage all show a less pronounced response to the oil shock if external feedbacks were excluded. Likewise, successive to an oil shock, the LDC debt problem worsens further if non-oil primary prices and the real interest rate are endogenized. Analogously, the real interest rate undergoes a further positive pressure if LDC debt and LDC aggregate demand are allowed to respond.

However an important qualification needs to be made with regard to the real interest rate: simulations show that the latter absorbs some of the rise and much of the volatility induced by the oil shock on the Northern economic system but also reveal that this 'advantage' to the North is paid in terms of a consistently higher level of LDC debt and an increased variability of LDC aggregate demand.

5.7 THE IMPACT OF THE REAL PRICE OF OIL ON THE LOW-FREQUENCY MOVEMENTS OF THE ENDOGENOUS VARIABLES

The role of the oil price in shaping the world economy changed dramatically from the late 1950s to the early 1990s. In order to outline its long-term impact Table 5.1 summarizes the results obtained by decomposing the variance of the equilibrium paths of the main endogenous variables.

For all the variables the change of the equilibrium paths ascribable to the price of oil[1] clearly shows up in the last three

Table 5.1   Changes of the oil price and of some equilibrium variables
due to the price of oil (percentage)

	58–67 to 68–72	68–72 to 73–79	73–79 to 80–84	80–84 to 85–88
$po - p$	−21.260	111.796	76.287	−62.129
po	6.780	159.550	123.790	−43.580
U	−0.076	0.399	0.272	−0.222
$pn - p$	−2.531	13.311	9.083	−7.400
$w - p$	0.053	−0.279	−0.191	0.155
R	−0.516	2.717	1.854	−1.510
$s - p$	−8.3586	43.9648	30.0014	−24.4335
y^*	−0.227	1.194	0.815	−0.663

Note: variable definition in the data appendix

intervals of time comprising the two positive oil shocks and the
negative 1986 'shock'.

As far as the OECD rate of unemployment is concerned the
real price of oil is not the most important determinant. At most
it causes a rise of 0.4 p.p. of the equilibrium unemployment
rate in the second interval but even in this case the price of oil is
not as important as the tax policy or the productivity trends.

The impact on the real wage is also minor and even negative:
that is, once non-oil primaries, but particularly the real interest
rate, are substituted out in the steady-state equation, real
wages do not exhibit an effective resistance to oil price hikes.

On the contrary, the oil price is one of the major forces
shaping non-oil prices: in the second and third intervals of time
it determines, respectively, 13 per cent and 9 per cent rise of
the equilibrium path of non-oil prices.

Likewise the unfolding of the oil price is crucial for the
development of the equilibrium real interest rate particularly
in the central periods when the trending factors cancel out.
Between the early 1970s and the mid 1980s the price of oil

induces a rise of even 3 p.p. of the equilibrium real interest rate; the same falls by 1.5 p.p. in response to the oil price drop of the late 1980s.

Finally oil price shocks strike heavily on LDC debt and determines a rise of its long-run value of more than 40 per cent; in the last span of time the decline of the oil price appears the only factor effectively helping the LDC external debt condition.

5.8   EPILOGUE

The key objective we had in mind when we started this research was to seize the links between OECD economic performance and primary commodity prices.

In responding to this main query, we necessarily touched other topics: the world financial market, the LDC external debt, the response of the LDC economy to the industrialized countries' performance, the role of industrial conflicts in the OECD labour market, the relevance of the real interest rate on the rate of unemployment, the degree of hysteresis

The model gained in terms of interest though it necessarily increased in complexity; nonetheless its basic features permit to retain a control of its working and in this lies its main strength.

Both in its theoretical and empirical version, the model remains a useful tool to tackle diverse issues. Among these we feel that the next one should be about macroeconomic policies; in particular we would suggest simulations concerning OECD monetary policy decisions and fiscal policy management. This further analysis would be valuable both to corroborate some of results obtained here and to answer more explicit economic policy questions.

Data Appendix:
Definitions and Sources

The main sources of the data are IMF and OECD statistics; in addition we used some data collected by David Grubb and explained in Grubb (1985). Since there is a slightly different country coverage between the IMF Definition of *Industrial Countries*, *Total OECD* and the countries entering Grubb's data set, adequate corrections have been made; these are explained in Cristini (1989).

a Index of technical progress.
Note: The index is derived as follows:

$$\Delta a = 1/sl\, \Delta\ln(Y) - [(1 - sl)/sl]\, \Delta\ln(K) - \Delta\ln(N),$$

where sl is the share of labour. The index of technical progress is obtained by assuming, arbitrarily, $a_{t=0} = 0$. Finally the index is smoothed by regressing a on a quintic trend and retaining the fitted values.

E Direct Total Debt of Central Governments of Industrialized Countries.
Source: IMF, International Financial Statistics.

F Oil Exporting Countries Wealth.
Source: IMF, International Financial Statistics.

H Average Hours per week.
Source: Grubb and ILO Year Book (YB).

i^l Long term nominal interest rate.
Source: IMF, International Financial Statistics.
Note: Aggregate figures are derived as a weighted average of individual country long-term interest rates using GDP shares in 1980 as weights.

i^s Short term nominal interest rate.
Source: IMF, International Financial Statistics.
Note: Aggregate figures are derived as a weighted average of individual country long-term interest rates using GDP shares in 1980 as weights.

K Capital Stock assuming a depreciation rate of 3.5 per cent.
Source: OECD National Accounts and elaborations.
Note: Aggregation has been made by summing over each country's capital stock. The latter was previously converted from national currency into dollars using the base year exchange rate. The calculation of capital

160

was made using TSP according to the formula $K_t = K_{t-1}(1 - d) + I_{t-1}$, where d is the depreciation rate and the capital stock is assumed to be measured at the beginning of the year.

L Total Labour Force.
Source: OECD Labour Force Statistics YB.

M Money + Quasi Money.
Source: IMF International Financial Statistics YB
Note: The index refers to Industrial Countries. Data are linearly interpolated between 1950–1955–1958.

N Total Employment.
Source: OECD Labour Force Statistics YB.

NC Number of conflicts.
Source: Grubb (1985).

P GDP Deflator.
Source: IMF, International Financial Statistics.

Pn Commodity price index excluding petroleum.
Source: UNCTAD, Yearbook of International Trade and Statistics 1979 1984 and updates.

Po Crude Petroleum price.
Source: United Nations Statistical Papers series M no. 82 and United Nations Monthly Bulletin of Statistics for update.

Pfe Price forecasting errors.
Note: Defined as the residuals of the following regression:

$$Pfe = \Delta\ln(P_t) - 1.14556\Delta\ln(P_{t-1}) + 0.39046\Delta\ln(P_{t-2}) - 0.2449\Delta\ln(P_{t-3})$$

where the coefficients on the right hand side are restricted to sum to one, that is inflation is neutral in the long run. This restriction is accepted as the standard error of the unrestricted equation (0.01344) is greater than the s.e. of the restricted equation (0.01332).

R Real long term interest rate deflated by 3-year expected inflation.
Note: Defined as follows:

$$R = i - [\ln(P_{t+1}) - \ln(P_t) + pfe_{t+1}]$$

S Developing Countries External Debt.
Source: IMF, World Debt Tables.

T = T1 + T2
where:
T2 Indirect taxes paid by households
Source: OECD National Accounts.
Note: *T*2 is defined as follows:

$$T2 = (HSS + IT)/HTR$$

where HSS = household contributions to social security, IT = indirect taxes, HTR = households total current receipts. HSS is not available for Australia, hence only IT has been considered.

T1 Tax on employment borne by the employer.
Source: ILO *The Cost of Social Security*, various years; OECD National Accounts.
Note: *T*1 is defined as follows:

$$T1 = EC/(IE - EC),$$

where $EC = SS + PE$, SS = Employers' contributions to social security, PE = Employers' contributions to private pension schemes and welfare plans (not available for Austria, Belgium, Finland, Norway) and IE = Employment contribution to income (ie Compensation to employees).

U Rate of unemployment.
Note: defined as $\log(L) - \log(N)$.

W Hourly Earnings.
Source: OECD Main Economic Indicators and elaborations.
Note: The total OECD has been obtained by weighted average; weights are the shares of employees in manufacturing in 1980.

Wfe Wage forecasting errors.
Note: Defined as the residuals of the following regression:

$$Wfe = \Delta\ln(W_t) - 1.35253\Delta\ln(W_{t-1}) + 0.65717\Delta\ln(W_{t-2})$$
$$- 0.30464\Delta\ln(W_{t-3})$$

where the coefficients on the right hand side are restricted to sum to one, that is inflation is neutral in the long run. This restriction is accepted as the standard error of the unrestricted equation (0.01422) is greater than the s.e. of the restricted equation (0.01406).

Y GDP at constant price.
Source: IMF, International Financial Statistics.

Yt GDP trend output.
Note: This variable is defined as the fitted values obtained by regressing log(Y) on a quintic trend.

Y* GDP at constant price of developing countries.
Source: IMF, International Financial Statistics.

Yt* Trend GDP of developing countries.
Note: This variable is defined as the fitted values obtained by regressing log(Y*) on a quintic trend.

Notes

Chapter 1

1. In fact the tested relationship is usually between output or GDP and the price of oil (see for example: Hamilton 1983, Darby 1982); the use of the rate of unemployment as the economic activity indicator is uncommon in this literature.
2. In this book, the term 'Industrialized Countries' is, for practical reasons, used interchangeably with 'OECD Countries', 'North' and 'Developed Countries'. Likewise, 'Developing Countries' and 'South' are used as synonymous. The actual country coverage of the blocs used in the empirical part is described in the data appendix.
3. Notice the implicit asymmetry accepted by Kaldor: the OECD reaction to primary commodity price shocks is sufficiently strong to revert the change of the terms of trade in face of a positive shock but not so in face of a negative shock. This is an interesting point since it points to the potential asymmetry of the alternating economic phases.
4. Usual North–South models are based on country blocs only and assume that the economic behaviour of each bloc is determined by the type of commodity it produces. In fact this hypothesis has recently become a limitation as many countries, traditionally classified in the Southern bloc, engage in manufacturing while important producers of primary commodities are located in the North. Unlike this traditional view, the model developed in this book emphasizes the difference between primary- and manufactured-commodity price formation.
5. A more debatable issue is the one concerning the long-run evolution of the developing countries' terms of trade. On this questions see Spraos (1980), Sapsford (1985), Cuddington and Urzua (1989). The early accepted view of a declining trend in the developing country terms of trade, originally advocated by Prebisch (1950) and Singer (1950) has recently been reassessed by Borensztein, Khan, Reinhart and Wickham (1994) and by Borensztein and Reinhart (1994) according to whom the downward trend of the real price of non-oil primaries can be largely interpreted as a permanent feature. A different view maintains that this conclusion is dependent on the time period considered; Powell (1989), for example, argues that terms of trade are nearly trendless once structural breaks are accounted for. We estimate the equilibrium non-oil real primary commodity price in Chapter 4.

6. The share of fuels in the OECD imports rose from 22 per cent in 1963 to 57 per cent in 1973; in 1987 it was back to 39 per cent. On average a barrel of crude oil costed $2.55 in 1972 and $11.28 in 1974; from 1978 to 1981 it rose from $12.94 to $34.74 whereas between 1985 and 1986 it fell from $26.98 to $13.82. Since 1991 crude oil costs around $18 a barrel. Recently, in front to a consistent fall of the oil quotation, dropped to 12–13 dollars per barrel, caused by overproduction and aggravated by the Asiatic crisis, Saudi Arabia, Venezuela and Mexico signed an agreement (22 March 1998) in order to cut their quotas of production. This agreement succeeded in moving the price back to around 15 dollars per barrel.

7. Using quarterly data from 1971 to 1980, Grilli and Yang (1983) find that the first oil crisis affected the markets for metals and non-food products for around two quarters; on the other hand food products prices seem to have responded more to the 1973 cereal crisis than to the oil price shock.

8. The Granger causality test is performed both between Δpo and Δpn as well as between $\Delta(po - p)$ and $\Delta(pn - p)$ from 1958 to 1988 where po is the log of the price of oil, pn is the log of the price of non-oil primary commodities, p is the log of GDP deflator and Δ indicates first differences. In each case the third lag on the dependent and independent variable is never significant. The F test for the significance of $\Delta(po - p)$ in the $\Delta(pn - p)$ equation is $F(2,32) = 7.833$; the test for the significance of Δpo in the Δpn equation is $F(2,32) = 5.51$; both are significant at 99 per cent. The reverse causality is never statistically significant.

9. See for example a recent investigation by Borensztein and Reinhart (1994) who find that the price of oil is a highly significant regressor in the non-oil primary price equation and considerably improves the overall performance of the model.

10. The primary commodity price is deflated by the OECD GDP deflator.

11. The real interest rate is defined as the long-tern interest rate minus the expected rate of inflation; the latter, in turn, is given by ex-post inflation plus price forecasting errors (see data appendix for details).

12. Notice that the primary commodity price indices used are already in 'OECD currency' as explained at the beginning of the next chapter. The exchange rate index used to convert nominal dollar prices into 'OECD' prices is an I(0) variable though it presents two major breaks in 1971 and in 1980–81.

13. A similar analysis is performed by B. Friedman and K. N. Kuttner (1992) to study the relationships between money, income, prices and interest rates in USA. Hamilton (1983) performs bivariate Granger-causality tests between the price of oil and six variables which approximate the macroeconomic system.

14. A confirmation of the exogenity of the price of oil is found by Hamilton (1983).

15. Gilbert (1989a) also come to the conclusion that is incorrect to specify short-run commodity price equations in real terms. This also accords with the fact that, in the short-run, commodity prices are essentially determined by demand and stockholding since supply is normally largely inelastic.

16. Moreover, total primary commodity and energy prices Granger-cause employment in Germany (with feedbacks) and in Italy; in the USA a significant impact of energy prices on employment is also present with feedbacks whereas no Granger causality between commodity prices and employment is found for the other countries considered. The relevance of the total primary commodity price index and of the energy price index on the rate of interest is significant and with feedbacks only for Japan.

17. The three oil shocks and the financial crisis of 1981 are typical examples.

18. I thank Giovanni Urga for this suggestion.

19. The four VAR systems are therefore defined as follows:

$y_1' = [(pc - p), U, R, t]$; step dummies at 1978, 1980, 1981, 1986.

$y_2' = [(pn - p), U, R, t]$; step dummies at 1978, 1981.

$y_3' = [(po - p), U, R, t]$; step dummies at 1981, 1986.

$y_4' = [(pn.p), (po - p), U, R, t]$; step dummies at 1978, 1981, 1986

In each case the constant and the step dummies enter as unrestricted; each variable, except constant, dummies and trend, enters the system with 1 lag: this length was determined according to standard tests (see Doornik and Hendry, 1994).

Chapter 2

1. The IMF aggregates country indices using a geometric mean where the weights are the time-varying relative shares of the series under consideration. This procedure may raise some questions regarding both the potential distributional effects of changes in the value of the dollar (Cristini, 1989) as well as the effects of outliers on the rate of change of nominal variables. The best way to take care of this would be to use PPP exchange rates but time series on these are not available for the span we consider (Gilbert, 1990).

2. A value added function is widely used in empirical studies (see for example Bruno and Sachs, 1985; Layard and Nickell, 1986; Layard *et al.*, 1991).

3. This assumption is discussed in detail in the next chapter.

4. In the empirical version of the model (Chapter 4) we will allow the mark-up to respond to primary commodity prices as they may be further indicators of the state of the cycle.

5. The analytical derivations and the theoretical values of the coefficients of all the equations presented in this chapter are provided in Chapter 3.

6. An exception is Manning (1991, 1993).
7. In the UK the same timing is clear also in 1989 when a new conflict upsurge coincided with rising inflation; the same was true, again, during the inflationary period of the early 1920s.
8. We may think of the real wage equation as already solved for the number of conflicts.
9. This point is to be taken up at length in Section 2.9 and again in Chapter 4.
10. Or the price equation upwards to point E or a mixed of the two operations.
11. See for example Stiglitz and Weiss (1981) and Fazzari *et al.* (1988).
12. As will be explained below nominal money supply is exogenous in the short-run but real money supply is endogenous in the long-run.
13. Indeed the real interest rate, defined as the difference between the nominal interest rate and expected inflation, includes, by definition, an unknown and uncertain component so that its computation is, to a certain degree, always arbitrary.
14. A collection of articles on the behaviour of the real interest in the OECD countries is edited by Mishkin (1993).
15. See, for example Cooper (1992). Real exchange rate policies and the management of imports have also been very important in shaping debts in many countries. Dornbusch (1986, Chapter 2) discusses the cases of Chile, Brazil and Argentina.
16. This decision was partly the consequence of considering the oil shock as a temporary event; at that time many people and economists thought the shock would had been short-lived (Cooper, 1992).
17. For most of the period considered in this study the oil market remained very far from competitiveness and was driven by the OPEC cartel decisions and political events. According to Gilbert (1990*a*) oil prices play the same role as good and bad harvests in the pre-industrial economies. The oil market re-gained some competitiveness only from the mid-1980s. For a survey of oil price models see Bacon (1991).
18. See for example Aizenman and Borensztien (1988), Borensztein and Reinhart (1994), Gilbert (1989a).
19. Since the dollar appreciation is usually measured relative to a basket of other OECD currencies, it is likely that heavily indebted LDCs further depreciate their currencies with respect to the dollar in order to gain competitiveness and raise their export revenues. Hence the level of LDC external debt could exert a negative influence on the real price of non-oil primary commodities expressed in OECD currency.
20. In the empirical version of the model the total primary commodity price index is always separated into its oil and non-oil components, i.e. into *pn* and *po*, in order to allow and test different elasticities to the two type of prices.

21. Let the production function and the trend production be defined as follows:

$$y = c_1 + a_1 n + d_1 k$$
$$\bar{y} = c_1 + a_1 l + d_1 k$$

Then, by subtracting trend production from actual production we obtain, on the assumption that technical progress and capital are constant at their trend values:

$$y - \bar{y} = a_1(n - l) = -a_1 U$$

22. In the long-run the slope of the North line may be negative if

$$\bar{d}_2 + \bar{d}_3 < \frac{\bar{d}_8}{\bar{b}_2 + \bar{b}_3}.$$

23. In general, the flatter the lines, the larger the impact of the shock on the rate of unemployment.

24. For this reason simulation exercises in Chapter 4 will be performed also for sub-sets of the model which alternatively exogenize some of the markets.

25. Again, this is true if $\bar{d}_{21}$ and $\bar{d}_{31}$ have the same signs as $\bar{d}_2$ and $\bar{d}_3$.

Chapter 3

1. Notice that equation (3.3), taking logarithms and re-arranging, can be written as: $y^e - y = \sigma \Delta d$, where small letters denote logarithms.

2. Using the first order condition obtained by maximizing the short-run ex-post profits with respect to output it is easy to show that $p_i = [1 - \frac{1}{|\varepsilon|}]^{-1} MC$, where MC are marginal costs and ε is the elasticity of demand.

3. See footnote 21 in Chapter 2.

4. In the estimated version of the model we verify whether primary commodity prices, as further indicators of the cyclical stance, may affect the price mark-up. This potential link is important since the use of a value added production function, by excluding raw materials, obscures an important link through which primary commodities may affect OECD activity (Bruno and Sachs, 1985; Muscatelli, 1995).

5. Notice that in a log-linear production function, the marginal product of labour is directly proportional to the average one. Hence, given the presence of cyclical variables, equation (3.4) may also represent a price equation derived on the basis of a mark-up on average normal costs rather than on marginal costs. The superiority of one type of mark-up rule over the other is not yet settled empirically or theoretically.

6. The rate of unemployment is approximately equal to $\ln(L/N)$ and $\ln(Y^e/L)$ is a measure of trend productivity on the assumption that expected demand is based on trend GDP.

7. As explained in the appendix to Chapter 1 OECD import prices are approximated by an aggregate primary commodity price index.

8. Lindbeck and Snower (1989).
9. See Oswald (1985) for a survey.
10. The result is obtained by approximating $\ln\left(\frac{(1-\theta)}{\theta}(1 - U_{-1}) + 1\right)$ to $\frac{(1-\theta)}{\theta}(1 - U_{-1})$.
11. In the empirical part we will not distinct between LDC oil-importing and oil-exporting countries but we will distinguish between oil and non-oil primary commodity prices; at this regard LDC terms of trade *vis à vis* OECD and *vis à vis* oil exporting countries are defined, respectively, as the ratio between the price of non-oil commodities and the OECD GDP deflator and as the ratio between the price of non-oil commodities and the price of oil.
12. A similar specification of the LDC debt function is used by Moutos and Vines (1989).
13. In this and in the following equation the convenience yield is omitted for simplicity. The convenience yield is related to transaction and precautionary demand; it is usually assumed to tend to zero as stocks approach high levels and to infinity as stocks tend to zero. The convenience yield assures positive stocks even when the circumstances are not favourable to speculative storage, that is, when the expected return is negative.
14. The storability of a commodity should be considered together with the elasticities of its demand and supply. Whereas supply is assumed to be almost perfectly elastic in the long-run for all commodities, in the short-run the elasticity of supply may vary; likewise the elasticity of demand may differ according to the use of the commodity: private consumption, generally related to a permanent income hypothesis is much less erratic than private investments. These different elasticities, in conjunction with the commodity's degree of storability may produce different response of the commodity price to shocks (Gilbert, 1990a).
15. See however Deaton and Laroque (1990).
16. Cristini (1989) discusses the effects of considering commodity prices in OECD currency.
17. This is necessary for various reasons: some commodities may not be storable, markets may not be efficient, available prices are trade prices rather than market prices.

Chapter 4

1. Data on benefits are not available for the relevant span and country coverage and do not appear in the wage equation.
2. Other authors favour this distinction. Gilbert (1990a), for example, finds that inflation in the largest OECD countries responds more forcefully to non-oil than to oil shocks although the shape of the two multipliers is very similar.

3. The standard error of the wage equation was significantly lower when using the aggregated index than when using the oil component alone.
4. On the presence of the real interest rate in the wage equation see Manning (1991, 1993). As discussed in the previous chapter the direction of the real interest rate effects in the price mark-up is also controversial.
5. Such a link was suggested in the theoretical equation; a similar possibility is also viewed by Moutos and Vines (1989).
6. Before arriving at the final specification of the LDC debt equation we also tested a structural break in 1981, as well as the relevance of the OECD rate of unemployment to seize OECD economic activity in place of y. Other acceptable specifications, which included the OECD rate of unemployment but hardly any change of regime did not affect the dynamics substantially (the oil shock simulations, for example, were always very close to those reported here) but usually showed excessive levels of the LDC external debt in the long-run equilibrium solution.
7. The insignificance of the real interest rate does not depend on the inclusion of the debt variable: this was tested by replacing the real debt with the real interest rate. The evidence about the significance of the interest rate in the primary commodity price equation is still unresolved: although some studies find a significant negative sign (Beenstock, 1988; Petersen and Srinivasan, 1995) others fail to find a robust link (Enoch and Panic, 1981; Winters, 1987; Gilbert and Palaskas, 1989; Vines and Ramamijam, 1988; Cristini, 1989, 1995a, b). In fact Gilbert (1990a) cites an invariably positive coefficient of the real interest rate indicating a possible simultaneity arising out of Government or Central Bank responses to inflationary pressures.
8. Since it is our objective to pursue an analysis beyond the partial equilibrium, we find it more effective to comment on the behaviour of the *system* in different contexts (long-run, short-run, simulative) rather than adopting a variable by variable description; the reader interested in the single variable behaviour can easily find the relative paragraphs in the following sections in the text.
9. In fact all lines depicted are derived from the overall estimated model; hence the conditioning on external markets has only instructive purposes as the values used to substitute for the endogenous variables are the average estimated ones and not the historical ones; in this way the values resulting from the intersection of the lines are the long-run overall equilibrium ones. True partial equilibrium models are used in the simulation exercises to assess the role of the different markets.
10. As far as the oil price shock is concerned, the final impact on U with and without financial market feedbacks is not definite 'a priori' as an oil shock rises the intercept of the South line and decreases that of the North line. This point is taken up again in Section 4.10 using simulation exercises.

1. The same figures also plot the simulated values (those obtained by simulating the model on historical values).

2. This finding, together with the downward trend visualized in the equilibrium path of real primary commodity prices (Figure 4.7a) supports the view of some permanent feature in the declining developing country terms of trade.

3. Given the presence of wage and price forecasting errors and of nominal variables, this position is not an equilibrium one. The short-run equilibrium path, defined in Chapter 2 as one in which there are no forecasting errors but there may be short-run demand factors, is derived in the next section.

4. In 1961,1963,1967,1968,1970,1971,1972,1974,1975,1976,1977,1980,1981, $\Delta U > 0$ and $U < U^*$; in 1984,1985,1987,1988 $\Delta U > 0$ and $U < U^*$.

5. The short-run equilibrium is obtained from the steady-state model where ΔU, Δy and Δy^* are additional regressors of the steady-state equations. These variables enter in the real interest rate equation, the primary commodity price equation and the two GDP equations. The short-run equilibrium so computed is characterized by the following sample average values: $U = 0.0491, (w - p) = -0.0818$, $NC/N = 0.0419, y = 4.398, y^* = 4.2089, (s - p) = -4.3646, (pn - p) = -0.2804, R = 0.1684$. Notice in particular that, since $U^{S*} < U^*$, in the sample period considered the problem of hysteresis was not probably wide-spread.

6. The short-run lines are not depicted since they are indeed very close to the long-run ones.

7. These regressions are the empirical analogies of equations (2.30), (2.31) and (2.32). The changes of production function elements that appear as additional explanatory variables enter the equation because of the substitution of Δy with ΔU using the production function.

8. The dynamic version of the model includes both short-run factors and adjustment processes; the so-called augmented long-run excludes the effects of the adjustment processes but retains those of short-run factors; finally the long-run model excludes both adjustment processes and short-run factors.

9. For variables defined in logarithms, the multipliers, multiplied by 100, give the percentage change of the variable induced by a doubling of the oil price; analogously, for the rate of unemployment and the real interest rate the multipliers show, once multiplied by 100, the percentage point change of these variables.

20. This rise may appear too little; however one has to consider that the first oil shock determined a *four-fold* use of p_0 whereas we simulate a twofold rise.

21. We have experimented with all possible sequences but no important differences emerged. See Cristini (1996).

Chapter 5

1. Since we are looking at an equilibrium context the oil price is the only component of the aggregate commodity price; the non-oil one, being endogenous, has been substituted out.

References

Aizenman, J. and Borensztein, E. R. (1988) 'Debt and Conditionality under Exogenous Terms of Trade Adjustments', *IMF Staff Papers*, 35, December, 686–713.

Ashenfelter, O. and Johnson, G. (1969) 'Bargaining Theory, Trade Unions and Industrial Strike Activity', *American Economic Review*, 59.

Bacon, R. (1991) 'Modelling the Price of Oil', *Oxford Review of Economic Policy*, Summer, 7, n. 2, 17–34.

Banerjee, A. and Urga, G. (1995) 'Looking for Structural Breaks in Co-Integrated Systems', mimeo.

Banerjee, A., Lumsdaine, R. L. and Stock, J. H. (1992) 'Recursive and Sequential Tests of the Unit-Root and Trend-Break Hypothesis: Theory and International Evidence', *Journal of Business and Economic Statistics*, 10.

Barro, R. J. and Sala-i-Martin, X. (1990) 'World Real Interest Rate', *NBER*, 3317.

Bean, C. R. (1994) 'European Unemployment: A Retrospective', *European Economic Review*, 38, 523–534.

Beckerman, W. and Jenkinson, T. (1986) 'What Stopped the Inflation? Unemployment or Commodity Prices', *Economic Journal*, 96, 39–54.

Beenstock, M. (1987a) 'An Aggregate Model of Output, Inflation and Interest Rate of the Industrialized Countries', Centre for Economic Policy Research D.P., no. 167.

Beenstock, M. (1987b) 'The Balance of Payments of Oil-Importing Developing Countries: An Aggregate Econometric Analysis', Centre for Economic Policy Research D.P., no. 165.

Beenstock, M. (1988) 'An Econometric Investigation of North–South Interdependence'. In Currie, D. and Vines, D. (1988) *Macroeconomic Interactions Between North and South*, Cambridge University Press.

Blanchard, O. and Summers, L. (1986) 'Hysteresis and the European Unemployment Problem', *NBER Macroeconomic Annual*, 15–77.

Blank, R. (ed.) (1994) *Social Protection Versus Economic Flexibility. Is There a Trade-off?*, NBER, University of Chicago Press.

Borensztein, E. and Reinhart, C. M. (1994) 'The Macroeconomic Determinants of Commodity Prices', *IMF Staff Papers*, 14(2)., 236–261.

Borensztein, E., Khan, M. S., Reinhart, C. M. and Wickham, P. (1994) 'The Behavior of Non-Oil Commodity Prices', *IMF Occasional Papers*, no. 112, August.

Breusch T. S. (1978) 'Testing for Autocorrelation in Dynamic Linear Models' Australian Economic papers, 17, 334–355.

Brown, G. (ed.) (1991) *OPEC and the World Energy Market. A Comprehensive Reference Guide*, Longman Current Affairs.

Bruno, M. and Sachs, J. (1985) *The economics of worldwide stagflation*, Harvard University Press, Cambridge, MA.

Chambers, R. G and Just, R. E. (1979) 'A Crtique of Exchange Rate Treatment in Agricultural Trade Models', *American Journal of Agricultural Economics*, 61, 249–57.

Cooper, N. C. (1992) *Economic Stabilization and Debt in Developing Countries*, MIT Press, Cambridge, MA.

Cristini, A. (1989) *OECD Activity and Commodity Prices*, DPhil Thesis, Oxford.

Cristini, A. (1995a) 'Primary Commodity Prices and the OECD Economic Performance', *European Economic Review*, 39, 83–98.

Cristini, A. (1995b) 'Economic Activity and Commodity Prices: Theory and Evidence'. In Vines, D. and Currie, D. (eds) *North–South Linkages and International Macroeconomic Policy*, Cambridge University Press.

Cristini, A. (1996) 'World Economy and Primary Commodity Prices' Monography n. 1, Dept. Economics, University of Bergamo, Bergamo.

Cuddington, J. T. and Urzua, C. M. (1989) 'Trends and Cycles in the Net-Barter Terms of Trade: A New Approach', *Economic Journal*, 99, June, 426–442.

Darby, M. (1982) 'The Price of Oil and World Inflation and Recession', *American Economic Review*, September, 12, 738–751.

Deaton, A. and Laroque, G. (1990) 'On the Behaviour of Commodity Prices', Princeton, mimeo.

Doornik, J. and Hendry, D. (1994) *PcFIML 8.0 Interactive Econometric Modelling of Dynamic Systems*, Institute of Economics and Statistics, Oxford.

Dornbusch, R. (1983) 'Flexible Exchange Rate and Interdependence', IMF Staff Papers.

Dornbusch, R. (1984) 'The Effects of OECD Macroeconomic Policies on Non-Oil Developing Countries: A Review'. In Colaco, F. and Van Wijnbergen, S. (eds) (1986) *International Capital Flows and the Developing Countries*.

Dornbusch, R. (1986) *Dollar, Debts and Deficits*, Leuven University Press, Leuven.

Enoch, C. and Panic, M. (1981) 'Commodity Prices in the 70s', *Bank of England Quarterly Bulletin*, 42–53.

Fazzari, S., Hubbard, R. and Petersen, B. (1988) 'Financing Constraints and Corporate Investments', *Brookings Papers on Economic Activity*, 1, 141–195.

Fisher, I. (1930) *The Theory of Interest*, Macmillan, New York.

Fitoussi, J-P. and Phelps, E. (1986) 'Causes of the 1980s Slump in Europe', *Brookings Papers on Economic Activity*, 2, 487–520.

Fitoussi, J-P. and Phelps, E. (1988) *The Slump in Europe*, Basil Blackwell, Oxford.

Friedman, B. and Kuttner, K. N. (1992) 'Money, Income, Prices and the Interest Rates', *American Economic Review*, June, 82, 472–492.

GATT *Le Commerce International* 1987–88, 1990–91.

Gilbert, C. (1973) 'Buffer Stocks, Exchange Rate Changes and Inflation', Oxford, mimeo.

Gilbert, C. (1987) 'The Impact of Exchange Rates and Developing Country Debt on Commodity Prices', *Applied Economics Discussion Papers*, University of Oxford, 30, June.

Gilbert, C. (1988) 'The Dynamics of Commodity Stocks and Prices and the Specification of Econometric Commodity Price Models', Institute of Economics and Statistics, University of Oxford, mimeo.

Gilbert, C. (1989a) 'The Impact of the Exchange Rate and Developing Country Debt on Commodity Prices', *Economic Journal*, 99, 773–84

Gilbert, C. (1989b) 'Modeling Primary Commodity Prices Under Rational Expectations', Report to the World Bank, International Commodity Division, mimeo.

Gilbert, C. (1990a) 'Primary Commodity Prices and Inflation', *Oxford Review of Economic Policy*, 6(4), 77–99.

Gilbert, C. (1990b) 'The Response of Primary Commodity Prices to Exchange Rate Changes', Queen Mary and Westfield College, London, mimeo.

Gilbert, C. and Palaskas, T. (1990) 'Modelling Expectation Formation in Primary Commodity Markets', D.P. 192, Economic Department, Queen Mary College, University of London, also in Winters, L. A. and Sapsford, D. (eds) *Primary Commodity Prices: Economic Models and Policy*, Cambridge University Press.

Godfrey, L. G. (1978) 'Testing for Higher Order Serial Correlation in Regression equations When the Regressors include Lagged Dependent Variables; *Econometrica*, 46, 1303–1310.

Grilli, E. R. and Yang, M. (1983) 'Real and Monetary Determinants of Non-Oil Primary Commodity Price Movements'. In Kregel, J. A. (ed.) *Distribution, Effective Demand and International Economic Relations*, Macmillan, London.

Grubb, D. (1985) 'The Revised OECD Data Set', Centre for Labour Economics, W.P. 781, London.

Gustafson, R. (1958) 'Implications of Recent Research on Optimal Storage Rules', *Journal of Farm Economics*, 40, 290–300.

Hamilton, J. D. (1983) 'Oil and the Macroeconomy since World War II', *Journal of Political Economy* 91(2), 228–248.

Hendry, D. (1988) 'The Encompassing Implications of Feedbacks Versus Forward Mechanisms in Econometrics', *Oxford Economic Papers*, 40, 132–149.

Hendry, D. (1989) *PC-GIVE: An Interactive Econometric Modelling System*, University of Oxford.

Hendry, D. and Richard, J. F. (1983) 'On the Formulation of the Empirical Models in Dynamic Econometrics', *Journal of Econometrics*, 20, 3–33.

Hicks, J. R. (1963) The Theory of Wages, London.

IMF *World Economic Outlook*, various issues.

IMF *International Financial Statistics, Supplement on Trade Statistics* various issues.

Johansen, S. (1988) 'Statistical Analysis of Cointegration Vectors' *Journal of Economic Dynamic and Control*, 12, 231–259.

Johnson, G. and Layard, R. (1986) 'The Natural Rate of Unemployment: Explanation and Policies'. In Ashenfelter, O. and Layard, R (eds) *Handbook of Labour Economics*, North Holland, Amsterdam.

Kaldor, N. (1976) 'Inflation and the Recession in the World Economy' *Economic Journal*, 86(344), 703–14.

Kalecky, M. (1938) 'The Determinants of the Distribution of National Income', *Econometrica*, 6.

Kanbur, R. and Vines, D. (1987) 'North-South Interaction and Cournot Control', *Journal of Development Economics*, 371–87.

Kennan, J. (1986) 'The Economics of Strikes'. In Ashenfelter, O. and Layard, R. (eds) *Handbook of Labour Economics*, North Holland, Amsterdam.

Keynes, J. M. (1939) 'Relative Movements of Real Wages and Output' *Economic Journal*, 49.

Labys, W. C. (1980) *Market Structure, Bargaining Power and Resource Price Formation*, Heath, Lexington, MA.

Labys, W. C. and Maizels, A. (1993) 'Commodity Price Fluctuations and Macroeconomic Adjustments in the Developed Economies', *Journal of Policy Modelling*, 5(3).

Layard, R. and Nickell, S. (1986) 'Unemployment in Britain' *Economica*, (supplement), 53, S121–S169.

Layard, R., Nickell, S. and Jackman, R. (1991) *Unemployment*, Oxford University Press.

Lindbeck, A. and Snower, D. (1989) *The Insider-Outsider Theory of Employment and Unemployment*, MIT Press, Cambridge, MA.

Manning, A. (1991) 'Productivity Growth, Wage Setting and the Equilibrium Rate of Unemployment', *NBER Conference on unemployment and wage determination*, Cambridge MA.

Manning, A. (1993) 'Wage Bargaining and the Phillips Curve: The Identification and Specification of Aggregate Wage Equations' *Economic Journal*, 103, 98–118.

Mishkin, F. S. (1981) 'The Real Interest Rate: An Empirical Investigation' *Canergie-Rochester Conference Series on Public Policy*, 15, 151–200.

Mishkin, F. S. (1993) *Money, Interest Rates and Inflation*, Edward Elgar, London.

Moutos, T. and Vines, D. (1989) 'The Simple Macroeconomics of North–South Interactions' *American Economic Review, Papers and Proceedings*, May, 270–276, 79, n. 2.

Moutos, T. and Vines, D. (1992) 'Output, Inflation and Commodity Prices', *Oxford Economic Papers*, 44, 355–372.

Muscatelli, V. A. (1995) 'Comment to A. Cristini Paper'. In Vines, D and Currie, D. (eds) *North–South Linkages and International Macroeconomic Policy*, Cambridge University Press.

Muth, J. (1961) 'Rational Expectations and the Theory of Price Movements', *Econometrica*, 29.

OECD (1983) *World Economic Interdependence and the Evolving North–South Relationship*, OECD, Paris.

Oswald, A. (1985) 'The Economic Theory of Trade Unions: An Introductory Survey', *Scandinavian Journal of Economics*, 87.

Paldam, M. (1989) 'A Wage Structure Theory of Inflation, Industrial Conflicts and Trade Unions', *Scandinavian Economic Journal*, 1.

Perron, P. (1989) 'The Great Crash, The Oil Price Shock and The Unit Root Hypothesis', *Econometrica*, 57, 1361–1402.

Pesaran, M. H. (1987) *The Limits to Rational Expectations*, Oxford, Basil Blackwell.

Petersen, C. and Srinivasan, T. G. (1995) 'Effects of a Rise in G-7 Interest Rates on Developing Countries'. In Vines, D. and Curries, D. (eds) *North–South Linkages and International Macroeconomic Policy*, Cambridge University Press.

Phelps, E. S. (1994) *Structural Slumps. The Modern Equilibrium Thoery of Unemployment, Interest and Assets*, Harvard University Press.

Phelps, E. S. and Winter, S. G. (1970) 'Optimal price Policy under Atomistic Competition in Phelps, E. S. *et al. Microeconomic Foundations of Employment and inflation Theory*, Norton, New York.

Powell, A. (1989) 'Commodity and Developing Country Terms of Trade: What Does the Long Run Show?', Institute of Economics and Statistics, Applied Economics discussion paper, 80.

Prebisch, R. (1950) *The Economic Development of Latin America and its Principal Problems*, New York, United Nations.

Ridler, D. and Yandle, C. (1972) 'A Simplified Method for Analyzing the Effects of Exchange Rate Changes on Exports of a Primary Commodity', *IMF Staff Papers*, 19, 559–78.

Rotemerg, J. and Soloner, G. (1986) 'A Supergame Theoretical Model of Price Wars During Booms', *American Economic Review*, June, 76, 390–407.

Rotenberg, J. and Woodford, M. (1991) 'Markups and the Business Cycle', *NBER Macroeconomic Annual*, 63–128.

Rotenberg, J. J. and Woodford, M. (1992) 'Oligopolistic Pricing and the Effects of Aggregate Demand on Economic Activity', *Journal of Political Economy*, 100, 1153–1207.

Sachs, J. (ed.) (1989) *Developing Country Debt and the World Economy*, NBER.

Sapsford, D. (1985) 'The Statistical Debate on the Net Barter Terms of Trade between Primary Commodities and Manufactures: a Comment and some Additional Evidence', *The Economic Journal*, 95, 781–8.

Sims, C. A. (1972) 'Money, Income and Causality', *American Economic Review*, 62.

Singer, H. W. (1950) 'The Distribution of Gains Between Investing and Borrowing Countries', *American Economic Review*, 40, May.

Solow, R. (1979) 'Another Possible Source of Wage Stickiness', *Journal of Macroeconomics*, 1(I).

Spraos, J. (1980) 'The Statistical Debate on the Net Barter Terms of Trade Between Primary Commodities and Manufactures', *Economic Journal*, 90, 107–28.

Stiglitz, J. E. and Weiss, A. (1981) 'Credit Rationing in Markets with Imperfect Information', *American Economic Review*, June, 71, 393–411.

Tarantelli, E. (1986) *Economia e Politica del Lavoro*, UTET.

UNCTAD (1987) *Handbook of International Trade and Development Statistics*, supplement.

Van Wijnbergen, S. (1985) 'Interdependence Revisited: A Developing Country Perspective on Macroeconomic Managment and Trade Policy in the Industrialized World', *Economic Policy*, November.

Vines, C. and Ramamijam, P. (1988) Commodity Prices, Financial Markets and World Income', mimeo.

Winters, A. (1987) 'Models of Primary Price Indices', *Oxford Bulletin of Economics and Statistics*, 49(3), August, 307–27.

Winters, A. and Sapsford, D. (1990) *Primary Commodity Prices, Economic Models and Policy*, CEPR, Cambridge University Press.

World Bank (1994) *World Development Report 1994*, Oxford University Press, New York.

Yellen, J. (1984) 'Efficiency Wage Model of Unemployment', *American Economic Review*, 74, n. 2, 200–205.

Index